Praise

"*Photography for Writers* is a treasure trove of ideas, prompts, and down-to-earth advice given in a conversational and uplifting style. A practical and vibrant guidebook to the intersections between writing and taking photographs, this volume is a must have for your shelf on the creative life."
SHAWNA LEMAY, AUTHOR OF *THE FLOWER CAN ALWAYS BE CHANGING* AND THE CREATIVITY BLOG TRANSACTIONS WITH BEAUTY TRANSACTIONSWITHBEAUTY.COM

"Finally, poetry for the photographer and photography for the poet! Whatever art you practice, the lessons in this book will inspire you to keep making—whether you need a reminder that imagery is the keystone or a lesson on how to learn from failure, this book will make you grow. Melanie is able to put the ineffable qualities of the creative process into simple, aphoristic lessons, illuminating the mystery of what we experience when we feel inspired. Melanie effortlessly wraps this how-to guide with personal anecdotes, highlighting that she continually practices the lessons she imparts while leaving us with the feeling that we are a little less alone in the creative process. Don't skip out on the prompts—I was shocked to find my poetry develop from an exercise found in the section on food photography (an art form I had no interest in before). Whatever your medium, this book will help your creativity flourish, with more than a few laughs along the way."
C. M. TOLLEFSON, HIGH SHELF PRESS

"If you're a writer (or photographer!) that's tired of the same old how-to books, then you're in luck. Melanie's advice takes you on a delightful tour of the creative world in a way you haven't seen yet. Her voice and ideas will spark ideas, you'll be laughing and learning but also producing! This book is a treat!"
KANDACE CHAPPLE, PUBLISHER AND WRITER OF *GRAND TRAVERSE WOMAN* MAGAZINE

"Finally, the book on *Photography For Writers* has been written. We now have all the ideas and inspiration we need to master the 'show don't tell' challenge. And of course, the author would be Melanie Faith, teacher, master creative, and master craftsman. As with her other excellent craft books, *In A Flash* and *Poetry Power*, she educates, illuminates and entertains. Whatever your creative challenge, using this guidebook with stimulating prompts and exercises, will direct you to where you need to go next."
MARI L. MCCARTHY, AUTHOR OF *JOURNALING POWER*

About the Author

Melanie Faith is an English professor, tutor, photographer, and freelance writing consultant whose writing has been nominated for three Pushcart Prizes. She loves writing and teaching in several genres, including flash fiction and nonfiction, poetry, creative nonfiction, novel-writing, and craft articles about the writing process. She holds an MFA from Queens University of Charlotte. Her photographs have been featured on literary magazine covers and on books of poetry. Check out Melanie's other two Vine Leaves Press craft books, *In a Flash!* and *Poetry Power*. In her free time she collects quotes, books, and shoes; learns about still-life photography and the tiny-house movement; and travels to spend time with her darling nieces.

To learn more about Melanie, visit: *melaniedfaith.com*

PHOTOGRAPHY FOR WRITERS

A Writer's Companion for Image-Making

MELANIE FAITH

Vine Leaves Press
Melbourne, Vic, Australia

Print Edition
ISBN: 978-1-925965-18-6

Published by Vine Leaves Press 2019
Melbourne, Victoria, Australia

Cover design by Jessica Bell
Interior design by Amie McCracken

A catalogue record for this book is available from the National Library of Australia

Table of Contents

To enjoy photographs described in this book as well as other helpful resources, please visit

melaniedfaith.com

"Make visible what, without you, might perhaps never have been seen."

Henri Cartier-Bresson

About This Book:

"YOU DON'T MAKE A PHOTOGRAPH JUST WITH A CAMERA. YOU BRING TO THE ACT OF PHOTOGRAPHY ALL THE PICTURES YOU HAVE SEEN, THE BOOKS YOU HAVE READ, THE MUSIC YOU HAVE HEARD, THE PEOPLE YOU HAVE LOVED." —ANSEL ADAMS

As I begin this introduction, I'm testing the strength of the string on my vanilla-caramel teabag. It's 2:10 in the afternoon. A little tug up, and the string pops above the mocha water in the blue mug. The string is fibrous, the heft of the pouch like the weight of marshmallows suspended from the ceiling on strings in Halloween party games where, as kids, we had to try to eat the marshmallows with hands behind our backs, unable to steady the string. A large part of the fun was laughing as the string wobbled out of control and the goopy mallow dangled, half-munched, just out of reach of our smiling faces.

The teabag, similarly, tilts and turns in a left-leaning pendulum above the steam-warm water. Like a diver, it plunges back into the water for another minute as the encased flakes produce a deepening dusk in the beverage cup. The steam swirls in a feathery plume above the ceramic mug lip.

Another minute, tops, and it will be ready to hold between two cold palms: sippable, scented, savory. An immersive experience. A time apart in the midst of the mania that is a modern workday.

Why all of this tea talk? Imagery.

Imagery is my jam. As a trained poet, I often think in symbols, motifs, and themes. In many ways, I prefer the big-picture and oblique to the stark and sparse. As a prose writer and teacher, one of the easiest and most thoughtful ways to underscore ideas is through the creation of vibrant, concrete metaphors and similes. Tea is tea (duh!), but it is also (like all of us) more than the sum of its parts. It means something at once communal and individual, even for people who hate tea and never drink it (here's looking at you, coffee drinkers).

Imagery's razzle-dazzle isn't limited to objects or people, though; it can encompass settings, conflict, tension, and more—just like its artistic cousins, the written arts.

In fact, the very pairing of two of my favorite art forms—creative writing and photography—sparked the impetus for this book. About a year ago, I had an epiphany for a new class I wanted to create. I'd just had a few more photographs accepted for publication in a literary magazine; my photography has been featured in literary journals since 2006 and on a few book covers since 2009ish. I've found my photography projects to be not only relaxing play but also an enhancement and an encourager for my writing process.

Wouldn't it be cool to teach the art of taking creative photos, just like I've been teaching the art of creative writing? No sooner did the idea zing through my mind than I set to typing a syllabus. What can I say? I'm a vivacious Type A.

Most of the writers who I know and teach in both

poetry and prose are avid photographers, even if they don't label themselves that. Photos of landscapes, loved ones, and selfies abound on the social media threads I follow, and website visuals also flourish. Many friends who have published work in literary magazines and websites have also submitted photos or other visual arts (including painting and collage) for publication as well.

What's the common ground between verbal and visual arts? Say it with me: imagery. You've got it.

I pitched the idea of a Photography for Writers class to my editors, who enthusiastically supported my new brainchild. While researching for a text for my new class, I came across a discovery (gulp): there were lots of books about creativity for writers (my own book-shelves happily sag with them) and oodles of books for budding photographers, but not much that focused on combining the two, and none that approached photography specifically from the way a writer thinks and creates while exploring a subject.

Aha! No text? No problem. I'd just write my own handouts and compile my own list of resources I'd found helpful for the intersection of my writing and visual-arts practices and submitting-work adventures.

I offered the first Photography for Writers course online for four weeks in April 2018. It was such a pleasure to share photobug tools, writing-imagery tips, and the marvelous photos we'd created during our weeks together that I immediately signed up to teach it again. I'll be teaching it for a third time, and I'm sure not the last. The feedback on my initial handouts was so supportive and encouraging that I've included several of them in this book—expanded and with the addition of a survey aimed to inspire and inform you about your own image-making preferences in both media.

My intention for this book is that you explore it at your own pace and with your own image-making growth at the forefront. While the text may be read chronologically by the divided three sections, "Section One: Inspiration Station—Sparking Ideas and Chugging Forward," "Section Two: Practical Craft Tips and Topics: The Intersection of Writing and Photography," and "Section Three: Getting Your Art out There" (a sharing, publishing, and marketing section), I know that my fellow creatives are each individuals and may choose to dip into and out of sections, which is another excellent way to approach life, learning, and artistic development. Go for it!

This book will *not* teach you F-stops or aperture or shutter speeds. It will *not* teach you camera settings. In fact, unlike many resources for photographers, this one will mostly be tech-jargon free. (Don't worry—there are oodles of books and websites for photographers that already explain all of the tech aspects you'd ever want to know; I include some great resources at the end of this book, in fact.)

Yeah, alright, you may be thinking. *So why read this thing?*

This book *will* enhance your creativity. It *will* meet you where you are as a thinker and a maker and enhance the talents of interpreting your world that you already possess. This book *will* offer practical yet imaginative ideas for developing everything from a single print to a photo series. It will teach you about taking the subject matter that appeals to you and creating imagery that communicates your personal and professional ideas to a waiting audience and then how to share (or selectively share) and market that photographic work to a waiting audience.

I've designed *Photography for Writers* to encompass writers whose photography is at all levels—from complete beginner to already-published and/or professional. Other than a camera, you don't need fancy equipment or even the newest software. Two of my DSLR (digital single-lens reflect) cameras are five or six years old, and I used one version of Photoshop for almost ten years before upgrading in 2017, all the while producing fine-arts photographs and developing my skills in both of my art forms.

As I've told the students in my workshops, with today's technology, a camera phone is another awesome way to practice developing your photography muscles; the quality of shots from cell phones rivals just about any camera I've ever seen or owned.

For writers who like their old-school analog (non-digital) cameras—I haven't forgotten about you, and I also applaud you; I have a chapter about several techniques and genres of photography that are making a resurgent comeback among storytellers of all ages. Or, what if you just want to use a blend of cell phone, analog, and digital cameras or alternate styles based on the project? Kudos! Why not? The tips and suggestions in this book work well, whatever your equipment.

Each chapter ends with a *Try this Prompt* exercise. I

wrote these thematic "assignments" to spark artmaking. Some of the prompts involve writing, many involve photographing, and oodles of others involve both arts. There's also a Thirty-One-Day Word Prompt List with several great ideas for how to get the most image-boosting from a daily creativity challenge. As always, the prompts and exercises are on-subject and yet general enough to get your own wheels turning. You might even choose to repeat your favorite exercises more than once or twice over a period of weeks or months to compare and contrast your growth as an artist.

Whether used singularly, in pairs, or in workshops or clubs, this book is meant to be interactive and encouraging for your Muse. It's my great hope that you find that one art enhances and speaks to the other, whether in ink and syllables or pixels and prints, or (why not?) a mixture of the two.

I suggest setting aside a separate writing notebook or daily journal in which to jot notes for future photos and photo shoots as well as to complete the *Try this Prompt* exercises. I often use spiral-bound journals, as they open easily and travel lightly in my purse or teaching satchel. You might also use a Word document with its own file name, if that's your preferred drafting method. It's handiest to have all of your musings in one place or file for later rereading and adding inspiration for projects.

So grab your journal or keyboard and your favorite camera and delve into an image-enhancing journey you're not soon to forget. Let's go!

But first—I've got some vanilla-caramel deliciousness to devour.

Section One: Inspiration Station —Sparking Ideas and Chugging Forward!

"Um … Um … I don't know."

Last night, the phone rang on my night off. My two darling nieces were on the other end. Cora Vi, who is almost six, began the conversation with a jot of news about school and a warm, bright, dainty hello. Halfway through the second or third sentence, another voice came on the line: my younger niece, Sylvie Ro.

My birthday-twin younger niece, three-and-a-half years old, adores talking on the phone. It took a while for both of my nieces to understand the concept of calling a cell phone that didn't have an image of my moving face on the other end (we often video-chat). Once they understood that I couldn't see their movements—that this was a voice-only kind of call—Sylvie, my verbal social-butterfly niece, took to the concept like a fish to water. Sometimes, when she sees my sister calling me, she asks (to my delight) to talk.

I love to "interview" this niece, as Sylvie Ro gives the most entertaining of answers, and I can tell that she adores having someone ask her opinions and thoughts about many subjects (as do many of us—hello, social media).

We chat about one of her favorite topics first: "What did you eat for dinner today?"

"Thai Kitchen … noodle take-out and [some word that is garbled over the phone line]."

"That sounds delicious. Did it make your tummy happy?"

"Yes! So good. I love it."

"Great! I haven't had Thai food in too long; maybe when I come to visit this summer, we'll get some. Can you guess what *I* had for dinner?"

"Um … um … (insert long silence here) cereal!"

"Nope, no cereal, although I like cereal. I'll give you a hint. It was one of your favorites and you put it on bread."

"Um … jelly? I think it jelly!"

"Close … but it's made from a nut, all ground up."

"Um … um … peanut butter san-dich."

"Yes! You like peanut butter sandwiches, don't you?"

"Um-hmm … yes, but it better on toast or bagel."

"That's very true; it is," I assent, imagining the serious look she gets on her face when discussing food. I can hear her playing with some kind of toy that she appears to be dragging across a surface (the wooden floor?) while she chats, so I keep the chat rolling.

"I heard you went tubing the other day. That sounds like a lot of fun!" I chirp. Although I haven't been tubing since high school, I don't tell her that. "Did you have fun?"

"Yes … a *lot* of fun! We went down this long [garble-garble sound] and then [some mushed word I can't make out]!"

"I'm glad you had so much fun, and that Cora Vi did, too. It's a good thing to have fun with friends and sisters," I say.

"Yeah," she agrees.

"I hear Cora Vi got a new scooter with two wheels and so you got Cora's big-girl scooter. That's really cool."

"Yes. I love it!" she says.

"I bet you wear your helmet, too."

"Yeah," she agrees.

"It's important to remember your helmet on the scooter. What color is it?" I ask, pretty sure it's one of Cora Vi's two faves: pink or purple.

"Um … um … I don't know."

"Is it pink, do you think?" I prompt.

"Um …"

"Or purple. I know you love blue."

"I love blue, yeah," she agrees; I imagine her bobbing her head. "Blue is my favorite, but sometimes gween or gold."

"But I bet Cora Vi's scooter that is now *your* brand-new-to-you scooter, since you're such a big girl, is purple. Do you think so?"

"Um … um … I don't know."

Truthfully, I love Sylvie Ro's willingness to admit she hasn't a clue. **One of the hardest things to communicate, as an artist, is the point where we're not sure of what we've just made, how it relates to whatever we've made before (or doesn't), what we should do with this new creation, if we should consider it practice and work on something new, or even what we should make next.**

It can be embarrassing and consternating to feel like every other artist's work is humming along with clear vision and no roadblocks in sight, while speed bumps seem to litter our paths. **Truth-be-told: it's perfectly normal for artists to falter (sometimes for weeks or months) right before a big breakthrough.** Keep on keeping on.

Over the course of practicing our craft, we certainly encounter many "Um ... um ... I don't know" moments. Haven't we all had the experience of writing a new short story, poem, or chapter in a novel and then rereading it later and thinking: "What will I do with this?" Or we've set up a flat-lay for a still-life photo or taken photos with a model or senior-portraits client and, after uploading them, noticed that the arrangement of items or the poses in some of the shots are awkward and didn't pan out. **Now what?**

Don't make any snap decisions, hasty edits, deletes, or reshoots just yet. It can be tempting to erase and start over, especially when we're confused about what this new creation is or why it turned out differently than we anticipated. Don't rush to delete. Many times, we can use parts or concepts from one photo to inspire another photo later, or a passage from one story might teach us something about a character that we can use later. If the work is gone, we can't look back on it to reflect on or reuse it.

Accentuate the positive. As creatives, the internal editor's voice tends to be strong and harsh, and we can become our own worst critics. **Is there one passage or part of your writing or photo that worked well? Study that element more closely.** What do you like most about that element? **Research online what other artists have to say about this element of creation to**

get further ideas for making the good aspect even better in the near future. Interviews with photographers and writers abound (for free!) on the internet, especially in small literary magazines like *Orson's Review* that did an interview with me about my photography: orsonspublishing.com/blog/orsons-review-issue-one-interview-melanie-faith.

Take the pressure off. Give yourself room to think and to play. Every shot Ansel Adams took of Yosemite didn't make it onto a gallery wall or a coffee-table book. Every short story or poem your favorite writer wrote didn't get published in a literary magazine. Not every piece is a critical success or even a part of where your work is headed next, nor does it have to be. Part of the joy of creating is making something with few, if any, expectations. It's often when we relax into the unknowns that our work heads in exciting new directions that become more obvious over time. Yet we can't count on this being the case for each new work; instead, a better approach is to make work with as few outcomes in mind as possible (this isn't an on-the-job review) and allow the creation itself to emerge.

Try this
Prompt! What don't you know about your art form(s)? Pull up a photo you consider a flub and/or a writing draft you thought was boring and peruse for one favorable quality that you can praise. Write for ten minutes about how you could begin again with this wonderful snippet to craft a better creation. Feel free to sketch or outline ideas as they occur to you, even after the ten minutes. On another day, do a free-write or a photo shoot where you take these repurposed ideas for a fun spin. **No expectations; just explore.**

Recognizing Your Subject

This morning, I read about a visual artist whose professor assigned the graduate students to make artwork not with the lines of their pencils but using the thing itself. The artist decided to trace an ornate manhole cover she passed by on her frequent walks to her student studio. Borrowing two orange cones, she sat on the ground in the middle of a city side-street and traced away to her heart's content.

This example immediately sparked my own thoughts about recognizing a subject to pursue. Two nights ago, while waiting for take-out food in a diner's parking lot that has been a local burger palace since the 1970s, I turned my head to glance at the adjoining gas station's back lot and felt it. Halfway between an "I wonder" and a "yes!" crossed with a "hmm." I noticed two burned-out vehicles, one an old bread delivery truck—now rusted and windowless and with its side roller-wheel door long absent—and a pick-up truck nestled nearby, similarly oxidized and with gouged-out, gaping holes where the dash window and headlights used to be.

When I say I felt an immediate pull to this pile of perfectly parked rubble, I do not lie. If it were a cartoon scene, my eyes would have bugged out with love-hearts and I would have dashed out the door to explore. Instead, I sat and talked myself into it by talking myself out of it at first. I had never arrived at this burger place, mid-afternoon, and not seen at least three vehicles in the carry-out window and assorted other cars scurrying around. How was it so empty at this time of day? And if I got out with my camera in hand and stood in the path of who-knew-who passing by, wouldn't I look like a fool? This wasn't a vacation spot where I could angle myself in traffic's way (as, okay, I've done when visiting friends or family) to get the shot I wanted. Not planning on getting out of the car, I'd barely brushed my hair—which was slung into a sloppy ponytail tied with an elastic—and I'm pretty sure the T-shirt I wore (my favorite, with a snazzy "Read More Poetry" logo in blue on blue) had a hole in the armpit from some insidious moth in storage last year. And I hadn't been planning on taking lots of shots so, *dang!*, I'd only brought a point-and-shoot camera instead of my preferred DSLR with all of the lenses and fancifying mechanistic power. What kind of shot could I get from across a gravel lot with people passing by at any moment?

No matter. I talked myself back into it because, just gazing at that pile of weather-roughed metal, my mind would not let me let go of it. I knew without knowing that I could capture something about it that would resonate with viewers. And so, I zoomed through the car window. Several snaps later, unsatisfied, I took the food and gave in—I opened the door and ran for a quick series of five additional captures, yielding one intriguing shot. (Check out the PDF photo file at melaniedfaith.com/photography-for-writers for photo #1 and to peruse other photos mentioned in this book, organized chronologically by chapter appearance.)

I felt the peace of stasis descend. I had gotten it, something about it anyway and perhaps imperfectly, but I had made something (which I then submitted to a literary journal the next day).

How do we recognize our subject? I've heard artists describe it as a kind of euphoria. For others, it's a quiet "aha!" moment. Also, a kind of dropping down a rabbit hole into intense concentration, like love at first sight. (I feel this hushed, exultant feeling when chasing the spark of an idea in my writing and in my photography; one moment, it's an everyday, ho-hum time and then, it's like a curtain parts and an idea dangles like the Fleece of Jason—just there for the taking, but not for long).

Finding our subject is all of the things we are *not* encouraged to be in our daily lives. **Identifying our subject is *not* rational, analytical, methodical, patient, or consistent. You cannot set your clock by it, as my grandfather used to say. Instead, it is fire-in-the-hole, it is combustion, it is a knowing thought with the force of magnetism, and it is very, very short-lived.** It is jet fuel, ready for take-off, not thinking ahead to landing—and that is as it should be. My best pieces, whether writing or photography, have been impulses, gut hunches, and puttering around on a rare afternoon when I'm under-scheduled. This is yet another reason why I recommend to my students and clients the benefits of an afternoon off to dawdle and do a whole lot of nothing every now and again.

Rarely does my best work arise out of endless pre-planning and weighing options—by that point, the brain tires and flags. **There is much to be said, in creating art at least, for focusing more on the itchy instinct than the end result.**

Sometimes, our subjects make immediate sense: the gardener who takes photos of produce and flowers, the astronomer whose writing and paintings follow constellations. Many other times, though, our subjects catch us unawares: walking the dog through the neighborhood, in the limber stage right after yoga, driving carpool, standing in line at a food truck (or waiting at a drive-thru). **Luckily, we live in a time when awesome cameras on phones and highly portable cameras make it possible to follow those inspirations with precious little lag time.**

Keep in mind:

- **What you find resonant as a subject may change based on a myriad of factors, such as whether you are in new surroundings or your old stomping grounds, the setting and climate, the weather, even your moods** (I take far different subjects when I am in a giddy, glad mood than when I'm feeling contemplative, and that's okay).

- **The worst thing you can do is second-guess why you would ever take a photograph of such-and-such a thing/person/idea and why anyone else would want to look at or own such an image. Repeat after me: Why *not*?** As poet Sylvia Plath noted, "The worst enemy to creativity is self-doubt." Follow the hunch, take the photos. **The opinion that matters most while creating your photos is yours;** not your friends', not your parents', not your romantic partner's, your coworkers', or your fellow photographers'. If it gave you pause or caught your attention, that's reason enough to pursue the subject. I've seen amazing photos of subjects some might consider mundane, from clothes-pins to a kid's building blocks.

- **Subjects won't wait forever. If you hesitate or ignore your ideas, circumstances won't wait around for you.** Often, you have only one— maybe two, max—chances to pursue your shimmery subjects before they move or circum-stances change and the photo-that-could-be is gone forever. Keep practicing—in writing and in photography, the easy-to-follow subjects gener-ally only follow after taking many, many photos of so-so material. Ironically, good timing takes time to learn. The more you get the feeling and follow through with subject sparks, the greater the odds that you will produce resonant, mean-ingful art.

- **Many subjects are symbols in disguise. Part of the magic of photography is *not* overana-lyzing our choices in the moment.** When you find something interesting or worthy of a second glance, that's a good indicator that there's some-thing personal, cultural, regional, or otherwise connected to you and your experiences as a person and an artist. **Let the symbolic meaning arise later and secondarily as you scroll through your photo roll or share with friends or potential buyers.**

Try this Prompt! Write about a time when you second-guessed your subject choice. What kept you from immediately following your hunch about what could make an interesting composition? Note what you can do to tune into and follow your subject hunch the next time. For example, will you carry your camera with you on walks for finding inspiration in your community? Will you increase the numbers of photos you take to get used to pushing sub-ject doubt aside?

A Skinny Little Boy with Copper-Penny Hair

"DON'T ASK YOURSELF WHAT THE WORLD NEEDS. ASK YOURSELF WHAT MAKES YOU COME ALIVE. AND THEN GO AND DO THAT. BECAUSE WHAT THE WORLD NEEDS IS PEOPLE WHO ARE ALIVE." —HOWARD THURMAN

There goes a skinny little boy with copper-penny hair in a bowl cut, Austin Powers glasses, and a megawatt, yet authentic, smile. He looks around nine or ten, and he skims down the blue carpet with a pretty hound which remarkably resembles his handler with his auburn fur. The handler and the dog give a little skip in their step that makes the audience, both in person and via TV, smile.

I don't have sons or auburn hair or, come to that, a dog—but I like all three. The little boy reminds me of a cross between a friend's younger brother growing up (who now has two or three half-grown kids and a wife) and a character from a holiday movie I streamed online recently.

This televised dog show is a post-feasting Thanksgiving tradition for me and my folks. My sister got us hooked on watching it while she was in high school in the late '90s, and ever since, post-feast-plucked Thanksgiving carcass, gravy glob-spill-over cleanup, and dried dishes, we hurry to pillows and sofas to soak in the parade of pooches, called by class. We learn the name, the state, tidbits about the handlers and the pooches' parents, you name it. Dog after dog, we watch, riveted, as each class is called forward: the Non-Sporting Group, the Herding Group, the Working Group, the Sporting Group, the Terrier Group, and more.

This particular boy interests me not only for his resemblance and all-in innocence but also because his hometown is a rural map dot less than an hour from where I live. I sit on the edge of the sofa and hope aloud that he gets called forward for the final round.

While, *alas!*, the boy's hound doesn't get called forward for the final prize round this year at the National Dog Show from the Westminster Kennel Club in Philadelphia (it's been around since the 1800s!), I was drawn by the youngster's beaming enthusiasm that zinged through the screen. Here was a boy with a passion for this show; the announcer even notes the extra pep in his step as he skip-steps along the carpet.

Why do some images or subjects call to us while others don't? There are about as many hypotheses as there are subjects to pursue, including but not limited to:

- **Nurture:** Our families of origin instill it in us. Not a lot of choice here, but it certainly explains some of the wacky but delicious dishes I enjoy noshing—mm, Baked Bean Sandwiches, anyone? Grab some white bread slices (preferably a thick Italian loaf) which you'll coat with a thin veneer of mayo, sprinkle some baked beans atop, layer cheese (singlesyou know, the cellophane-wrapped kind, cut into two oblong pieces work best to get the ooey-gooey oven-melt going), and garnish with a dollop of chewy bacon. Set the oven to broil and wait for mere minutes while you salivate.

- **Geography:** Well, of course you like surfing; you grew up in Southern California or Hawaii or Florida. No wonder you love snowy Thanksgivings with those Lake Michigan or Lake Erie winters.

- **Education:** Liberal arts colleges (I attended two) are famous for encouraging a broad-based course selection in numerous non-major classes to create "well-rounded" individuals. Hey, ya never know when you'll need that Psychology of Underwater Basket Weaving seminar you attended. On a more serious note, we often stumble upon classes we never thought would recur in our lives, and yet, their influence ripples down through decades. (Here's looking at you, awesome Art Appreciation, Spring 1999 semester!) Most classes, seminars, and workshops teach a particular way of questioning and perceiving the world that influences what we are drawn to and, conversely, what confuses or repels us.

- **Friend-mily:** Those peeps you hang out with introduce you to oodles of life's options, from singers to movies to books to sports and hobbies that may never have crossed your radar before your friends became part of your posse.

- **Occupation Station:** Okay, so we don't all have our dream jobs, but there's a lot to be learned about ourselves and what we like and loathe from our job du jour.

- **Memory lane:** As with the peppy boy with his beautiful hound, some subjects remind us of people, places, and events we've known. While this can, admittedly, sometimes lead to nostalgia, it can also lead to some amazingly resonant art because memories trigger the passion, angst, and insights from hard-earned life experience. Conversely, bad experiences can help us to narrow or to steer away from various topics, or even to beeline straight to them as a vital part of the healing process.

- **Nature:** We are just inherently drawn to some things. Almost like breathing, we've always found trees compelling or empty buildings fascinating. When people think of you, they think of your panache for making brioche or pastries or kugel or latkes or chicken soup. It's your jam; why fight it?

Whatever compels us towards certain subjects and not others, it's clear that as artists we find connections (whether innate or learned) to certain topics that

inspire. Pierre-Auguste Renoir noted, "Art is about emotion; if art needs to be explained it is no longer art."

Yesterday, my university students and I were discussing, among other things, how we spend a lot of time with people telling us why something *won't* work and how things *shouldn't* be done, and yet we have other, often-unspoken, reasons for following the trajectory of what naturally inspires us. Shifting our focus from the naysaying to diving into the subject can lead to amazing projects.

Try this Prompt! Make a list of influencers in your life. Then take the imagery inventory at the end of this first section to discover the particular kinds of imagery that spark your Muse.

The Punch Line: Finding Photographic Resonance

"Knock-knock."

"Who's there?"

"Interrupting Cow."

"Interrupting cow wh—?"

"MOOOOOOOOOOO!" My six-year-old niece, Cora Vi, belts out the punchline with a gaggle of giggles unspooling. Although I've heard this joke a million (and one) times, I find myself laughing along with good humor.

This summer, both of my nieces are old enough to enjoy not only hearing jokes but making them up on the spot. I recall being in first grade and loving to stand on the woodpile while my dad split large chunks of elm for the stove, making up jokes.

"I have one for you," I say, pulling out the one kid joke I can successfully remember. A kid joke, in fact, that my Uncle D taught me once-upon-the-early-'80s.

"Okay," my elder niece says, a little smirk on her cute face as she leans in.

"Knock, knock," I begin.

"Who's there?" She's game.

"Banana."

"Banana who?"

"Knock, knock."

"Who's there?"

"Banana."

"Banana WHO?" she asks, a little more emphatically.

"Knock, knock," I snicker.

"Who's THERE?"

"Orange," I trumpet with a smile.

"ORANGE WHO?" she shouts.

"Orange you glad I didn't say banana?" I reach over to tickle her arm, but she wriggles away, giggling.

"My turn!" she says.

She then proceeds to tell her own jokes, all of which end with fruit, like grapes or apples, that make no sense with the aren't/orange pattern, but I see what she's doing and gamely laugh along.

The problem with the jokes I made up at Cora Vi's age and told my willing-to-listen-while-working Dad is that their set-ups often didn't match their punch-lines. Puns slightly off-kilter. Mis-recalled subjects. Pauses in the middle of trying to recall the right words, attempting do-overs. What can I say? It's a skill that runs in the family.

Often, as artists, we aim for the satisfying one-two punch that challenges our audience's perception and creates interest. One of the reasons why kids love jokes so much, other than shining in the spotlight and the natural satisfaction of making someone else laugh, is that jokes are a dichotomy: they both set up a pattern and tear down the pattern with innovation and the unexpected. In writing, something unexpected and (frequently) terrible has to happen to our protagonist in order for the character to act in unfamiliar ways that lead to growth. In other words: characters whose lives are always happy and easy are a snooze fest and no reader will keep reading about them.

Similarly, in photography, we need to set up certain parameters and then put our own unique spins to tear down those viewer expectations at the same time or else viewers won't find our work compelling or worth a second look.

The following traits of jokes apply well to our writing as well as to our photography.

- **Good jokes are specific.**
- **Good jokes focus on one subject.**
- **Good jokes show us a new or different side of something familiar.**
- **Good jokes upend our expectations and show us something about ourselves or others that we hadn't considered before.**
- **Good jokes are succinct and stand on their own. They make sense and create meaning as a unit, whether or not they are told as a series.**
- **Good jokes build quickly.**
- **No excess details. Good jokes don't have even one element too much.**

Now that my nieces are into jokes, I need to step up my repertoire. I have a horrible memory for punch lines. While I order a joke book or two, take the following prompt for a spin.

Try this Prompt!
Jot a list of three common subjects (for example: hair, a door, a yoga mat). Brainstorm for ten minutes how you might explore each of these common subjects in an unexpected way. What elements might you include in the photo to intrigue your viewers? What angle might you use? What one aspect of the common object might you highlight that will surprise viewers? Keep in mind that you might have to omit excess background or other objects from the frame. Take ten photos each of the three subjects. Pick the best one of each. Why is this one your favorite?

A variation on this exercise: Swap lists with a photography friend and have your friend choose the top three from your shoot while you return the favor for them. What surprising elements did this exercise bring out that created resonance in your three chosen photos?

Jolie Laide: Photographing the Unconventionally Beautiful

One of the few terms I remember vividly from my days as a French student is *jolie laide*. The literal translation of this phrase, *pretty ugly*, doesn't translate so lovingly from one language to the other! Who wants to be *very ugly*? In this case, the meaning is meant more as a compliment and refers instead to attractiveness in surprising ways: slightly crooked teeth, thin lips, a birthmark, or awkward, slumped posture. And yet, among the asymmetry or unfavored trait lies a beguiling personality, an allure that is, yes, both physical and emotional. She has her own style and viewpoint. The *jolie laide* woman appeals to others because of her unique qualities. She thinks and acts independently and idiosyncratically. *Jolie laide* includes the below-skin-deep characteristics that make up a person's overall appeal. More of the whole package than a quick glance of hot or not.

While I have mixed feelings about this term—there are inherent problems in such value judgments, especially of women's bodies (who is anyone to judge anyone else, especially on our physicality, which is quite often nit-picked to death and a struggle for women?)—it does bring up a compelling concept that translates well into photography: there's more to a subject than what meets the eye, even when you're using your eyes!

I had a blast teaching my first photography class this spring, and one of my favorite conversations focused on the unconventional things we find compelling to photograph. These might be subjects that you find yourself suddenly pulled toward when out-and-about with your camera and might hesitate, with a little *hmm*, before going with the hunch. One of my students found herself drawn to patterns of rust, another to rot and decay (such as flowers after their bloom). We noted taking photos of items left out in rain, snow, and other intense weather conditions. I mentioned my own interest in buildings and other architecture in various states of falling down or apart. While these subjects are certainly not human in scope, they fit nicely into the category of quirky yet compelling. (Check out the PDF photo file at melaniedfaith.com/photography-for-writers for example photos #2, #3, and #4.)

There will be a million-and-one photos of predictably gorgeous subjects that we all still like to photograph and should. I took thousands of photos of my nieces when they were babies and toddlers and I don't regret a single one, of course; same thing with documenting trees in all seasons.

Yet, documenting subjects considered quirky or offbeat can launch our artistic skills to a new level. Why not follow oddball or eccentric topics that tug at your Muse? Rather than questioning why a subject has appeal or if anyone else could possibly find the topic appealing, go for it. You are drawn to a topic for a reason. Yours might be the photos that encourage others to see the subject from a new angle or even to craft their own *jolie laide* images.

Try this Prompt! For twenty minutes, write about a time when you questioned or doubted your attraction to a *jolie laide* subject. Did you end up taking the photos or writing about the subject? Why or why not? Reflecting back, what can you take away from either capturing the subject or deciding not to do so?

Apply this lesson to a series of photos about the next unconventionally beautiful subject you photograph.

Tropey-Dokey: Enhancing Imagery with Tropes

12:30 p.m. was a sacrosanct time for my grandma and my mom. It was the starting time for their favorite soap. As in "their stories." Month after month, year after year, from two houses a half-town apart—both of which (for the '70s and '80s) used rabbit-ear antennas—they tuned in five days a week to follow the unfurling complications of characters both glam-tastic and down-on-their-luck in a fabled city that had the same name as a European city (which definitely upped the appeal factor).

These characters flirted, coupled, uncoupled, sought retribution in various flavors, recoupled, had children, had more divorces, had feuds with family and former friends, bought companies, sold companies, lounged by the pool, lounged with the pool boy, tangoed with the pool boy turned executive, had additional children, had paternity tests, had companies taken from them, and more. Lather, rinse, repeat.

Okay, so sometimes the plot lines were admittedly

fantastical—amnesia and never-before-mentioned twin sisters appearing, anyone? Still, the protagonists (and often the rascally antagonists, too) were likeable in their emotional conflicts and botched intentions. These characters' names and their antics were just as likely to turn up in my grandma's and mom's early-morning phone calls or end-of-the-day conversations as real-life cousins and friends. What's the appeal?

Soap operas, like most movies, plays, and visual storytelling, are based on comforting tropes, you know: those recurring motifs and literary devices that we can often foresee but still wait around to watch how it all shakes down anyway. Unlike learning calculus or molecular biology, we don't have to strain to notice bits and pieces of what it's like to struggle and to celebrate human foibles and small triumphs within the characters whose lives unfurl scene by scene, even if our own lives don't involve heirs/heiresses, ballrooms, or jet-setting.

Lest you think soap operas are solely low-brow and cheesy escapism, think again: tropes can be traced as far back as the ancient world. In Classical Greek, the term means, "turn," and is still used in modern Deconstruction Theory. Aristotle, in *Poetics,* discusses common tropes in tragedies and epics. Before I cause the need for No-Doz, I'll resist launching further into analysis. The important part about tropes is that although they might be borderline cliché, viewers, readers, and artists all relish the extended narratives developed using these recognizable patterns.

In short: tropes, my friends, are our friends.

As a freelance teacher, I work strange and flexible hours. I sometimes still turn on the stories for a burble of background hum; although, these days, I don't know who half of the characters are, why there's no longer a ballroom or café, and why most scenes take place in a set done up to resemble the living room of some mansion, but it matters little. There's a comfort level in piecing together what I do know while filling in the rest, like completing the outline of a jigsaw puzzle while answering emails or making lists for what I need to finish today for my various jobs.

It's not rocket science, but that's not usually what we need from the art we enjoy or the art we create—**art is the balance of tension between the familiar and the simultaneous need for escape from drudgery. Resonant art has elements of the recognizable as well as elements of transcendence.** Too much of one over the other leaves us cold, with no connection to the material. Too little of both, and it likely won't catch, much less hold, our attention in the barrage of sights, sounds, and events flooding our days.

Tropes might seem a shortcut, but they provide a meaningful jumping-off point for riffs on numerous human experiences.

Timeless, recurring tropes explored in the visual and written arts include:

- Misunderstood or conflicted protagonists, commonly in youth but other life stages, too

- Changes of personal or group identity, mistaken identity

- Changes of locale/geography, escape

- Love gained, love in trouble, love lost, love regretted

- Death and the dying process

- The un-suppressible secret

- The unexpected accident and its aftermath

- Retribution/Payback (whether delivered person-to-person or on its own)

- Changing seasons—both geographic and internal/metaphorical

- Rescue—of others, of self

- Reunions of individuals (former friends, former enemies) or groups.

Try this Prompt! Pick three of the above tropes. Jot ideas for ten minutes, without stopping to censor yourself, of how you might express these common tropes using your own unique talents and photo-taking skills. Consider locations or backdrops and possible props or subjects you might incorporate into each of the three tropes. Compare and contrast the notes you take on your chosen three tropes. Cross out the most-cliché description of the three, and then pick one of the other two tropes to make into a photo session or photo series. Go!

The Great Hide-and-Seek Expedition

"Where's Hyun-Seok?"

His roommate, a lanky kid from South America, gave a little smile that could mean complicity or could mean *that-roommate-of-mine-is-cray-cray* and a shrug of his shoulders from his desk. An electronic translator, various pens, and notebooks swarmed the pockmarked surface like constellations in a crowded sky.

Even at twenty-three, I knew the first rule of being an adult teacher or coach: you don't corner one kid to rat out another kid. There wasn't time for figuring it out, anyway. The number-one priority had to be: find Hyun-Seok.

It was 10:30 p.m. on a July evening. The thermometer hovered near a toasty ninety degrees while the air conditioning decided if it wanted to work, but that didn't mean my evening on the job was over. Far from it; I had dorm duty at the summer camp for international students where I was teaching American History. This was the cursory round to make sure everyone was in the dorm; at 11:00, I'd start the round for lights-out, which they'd sneak out on five minutes later to keep working on homework or, more likely, doing who-knew-what until midnight when I journeyed home.

At 10:30, it was time to peruse rooms to make sure none of my charges were roaming halls or setting fire to bathrooms—or each other—but instead were safely and industriously in their rooms, studying away (or at least giving a courtesy semblance of studiousness until I had advanced to the next room).

The girls' floor had made it through the check, no problem. A recent college graduate, I was still close enough in age to my students to have the same hair-style, jean style, and hopes for our futures; we were close enough in age to speak the same emotional language, too. The first boys' floor, too; easy, breezy check-ins—until Room 320. Until Hyun-Seok.

At eleven years old, he was whip-smart and intuitive. He was also the youngest camper, by four or five years. He was a foot shorter than the other kids, including many of the girls. In some ways, he was the group's class clown—making silly faces at dinner, doing impressions of TV characters (and, I'm sure, teachers), standing in the aisle during bus trips. In other ways, he was the camp mascot. There were pressures involved with being sent to an academic camp thousands of miles from home during school vacation, in a language in which your communication was little better than a five-or-six-year-old child's while your social standing among your peers wasn't much better. All of these students felt homesick, hormonal, and highly tired—who could blame a kid for wanting a little fun on an otherwise hum-drum weeknight? That's why some of us looked the other way when he went zipping down the hall with airplane arms, making buzzing noises. Or when he asked intrusive questions of fellow campers or, once, his counselor. It was just Hyun-Seok being Hyun-Seok.

The not-showing-up-for-check-in, though, was a new one, a potentially dangerous one. Nobody wants to call a parent to report their darling son has gone AWOL in a foreign country.

Thus began the Great Hyun-Seok Hide-and-Seek Expedition. Behind the desk. In the closet. In his room-mate's closet. Unzipping the two giant suitcases both had carried with them. Down the hall. In both bathrooms, all of the shower stalls (yelling into the bathroom first to ensure no one was scrub-a-dubbing in there). Downstairs in the lounge. Back upstairs in the empty kitchenette where a TV still droned an Austin Powers movie that was popular that summer. Upstairs to the third floor to check with another teacher—nope, nobody had seen Hyun-Scok.

Rule number two of being a teacher or coach: you do all you can possibly do before admitting things have gone out of control.

Think, think, think. I remembered security's number, but I couldn't recall if I'd seen him during afternoon activities or even during dinner. There was a phone in the lounge (this was in the days before everybody carried their lives on a cell phone). I thought about the woods that bordered several areas of campus. I thought about the sleepy town beyond it, where he was probably just fine, no problems, doing okay, and yet—there was still a lot he could get into with very, very limited English. My heart plummeted as I ran down the hall.

Back to Hyun-Seok's room. *Five more minutes,* I promised myself, *and I'll call security. I'll hand it over to them, before—. No, don't think that way. He's fine. He has to be here, somewhere.*

Again, I knew the quiet roommate would be no help. Again, perusals through both closets, behind the beds, the obviously empty suitcases, my pulse racing. I'd only been teaching professionally for two years; it would not look great to lose a student, and he could be in danger somewhere.

Maybe he fell and hurt himself after the baseball game and nobody noticed. Maybe … No, don't go there.

"Did you see him after the game?" I asked the roommate, trying to keep the frantic out of my tone. "Was he at dinner? Did you guys hang out during free time?"

My eyes landed on the dresser. Built like a tank, with long, slim drawers, it was probably older than I was. It couldn't be … he wouldn't fit. Or would he?

Top drawer: socks, underwear, who knew what else. Middle drawer: shirts, pants, a sweatshirt with the camp crest.

Bottom drawer: a curled-up eleven-year-old kid. "Su-prise."

His roommate was now howling with laughter; of course, he'd been in on it. I was howling, but not with laughter—with relief that I hadn't lost a camper and wouldn't have to call security or freaking-out parents. I still had a desire to crunch them both. I bit back the words of warning and managed to remove myself from the room without losing my cool.

Later—we're talking hours later—I would chuckle about it with a fellow teacher in the lounge as we sat grading assignments and planning for the next day's lessons. In fact, we'd start to howl laughing. Of *course,* it had been Hyun-Seok. Of *course,* he'd folded himself into a pretzel in the drawer. Of *course,* he'd waited it out to get the big laugh.

We tend to fight surprises, shoving them to the proverbial bottom drawer of our minds—seeing them as obstructions to what we want to accomplish as creatives. We promise ourselves we'll explore those other ideas later, when it's more convenient (as if there will ever be a more-convenient time without distractions or responsibilities). We go to photograph one thing and, unexpectedly, we see something else along the way that calls to us.

But there's no time! Or it's an inconvenient place to take pictures or to park! Or we've never photographed that thing before and don't know how to light it or even if other people would be interested. Why bother? A tiny part of us asks, so we rush forward with original plans, the bonus idea trailing us for a few minutes like a vapor until it's evaporated into a faint inner build-up of disappointment.

As a photographer and a writer (and, clearly, as a teacher), I've learned quite a bit from the unexpected and the inconvenient.

- **Hunches are there for a reason. They are your artistic instincts—don't overthink them.** You've been waiting all week for the lilacs to bloom so you can get the perfect picture of them, and the day is finally here. Except—you keep being distracted by the empty trellis across the garden. Why the empty trellis? The lilacs won't last long, and there's rain in the forecast for this afternoon, and …. No. Don't fight it. Get thyself to the trellis, stat. Take a few photos. The lilacs will be there in a few. Which brings me to …

- **You have five more minutes.** No, you don't have all day or even all afternoon to yourself, I get that, but you have time to explore just one more idea. Seriously. No, bosses don't wait indefinitely or even patiently. Neither do deadlines or children or spouses or … Then again, **adjusting your schedule, apologizing for being late, or taking a needed extension is far better than the accumulation of months' (or years'!) worth of turning your back on the intuitive nudges and sparks of ideas that are the great gifts of being an artist.** People who love you will get over it, and people who don't love you will adjust or deal with it. You can't explore every wild hair, but you deserve to listen to a few; it's how we make discoveries and breakthroughs. **Repeat after me: if I wait, it will never happen. Now is the time.**

- **Never shot this prop? Never tried this pose? Never wanted to snap this subject before?**

Opportunity knocks. Many of our best future photos are waiting in the novel and new. Yes, these first few images might flop, but then again, they might get us to where we need to go in the future. (See also: don't overthink it.)

• **Much of making remarkable photographs happens internally, before you even snap the shutter.** You know more than you think you do. You have more skills than you can imagine. You don't need to be perfect to craft a memorable image. Slightly blurry can be an aesthetic. Off-center can become remarkable. Odd to you may be unique and gaze-worthy to another viewer.

Try this Prompt! Write down one (or two or three) hunches and intuitive ideas that bubble up as you photograph what you'd planned. At the end of your session (or mid-way through—I dare ya!), explore one (or more) of the doesn't-make-literal-sense, inconvenient subjects or locations. Don't wait until another day. Go now!

At the end of the day, compare and contrast your first photos to the wild-hair images. What qualities do you like from each? Which shoot surprises you more, and why?

True North: On Mute-Buttoning the Inner Critic

A close friend alludes to finding True North in his latest social-media post. It's a fanciful phrase I haven't heard in a while, at least in the metaphorical sense, and it puts a smile on my face to be reminded. Today, on Christmas Eve, many of our minds are on the toy-toting famous denizen of the North Pole.

In a literal, sciencey-sense, True North is found with a compass. Whatever direction a person heads toward, once they find the direction of the North Pole, everything else can be figured out relative to knowing that one fixed detail. Just find North, and everything else falls into place.

As a creative, I'm more interested in the idiomatic use of True North, although the compass image remains pretty handy. A lot of being a maker involves intuition and, with just one tiny fixed idea, figuring out the rest during the creation and editing processes. There's a heaping helping of the unknown involved in both writing and photographing; we know this—we've *felt* this and *heard* this, both from others and ourselves.

In fact, as cynical and critical as our acquaintances might get, our own internal critics are usually crankier, more despondent, and even brutal. *This is stupid and trite. Don't show it to anybody; they'll laugh you out of the place. Smart people don't lay all of their cards on the table and share what they're really thinking. It's all been done before, anyway! What could you possibly have to say that's better than what's already out there?*

Sound familiar? We've all been there and pushed through to create more art. How?

- **Stick with the spark while creating.** Deep down, most of us get a kick out of the initial spark that sends us to the camera or page and then, just as easily as the idea appears, the fervor disappears and the doubts creep in. (See above.) Overthinking can derail your own train; keep chugging along.

- **No subject is too trite or covered too-often.** We don't expect sculptors to stop making sculptures of the human form just because we already have da Vinci's masterpiece, *David*, nor do we expect painters to stop painting night landscapes because we already have van Gogh's *The Starry Night*. **Each artist puts a unique spin on a theme or motif; you will, too. No one alive today or who has ever lived has had quite the same collection of life experiences as you; your art is bound to reflect your own distinctive contributions.**

- When I stop to reflect on my own works-in-progress, I like **the compliment sandwich approach** that I often offer my students and clients—feedback on something that's working well, a suggestion or two on what could be better, and more praise on something that's well done. Then, I shove it all aside and keep working.

- As my Grannie Lou used to say, kindness begins at home. **If you wouldn't say it to a friend about their piece, don't say it to yourself.** Treat your own Muse with the same kind of respect and care you offer others. Most of us are far harder on our own works-in-progress than we would be to anyone else's, even if we're part of a workshop, teaching circle, or other group where criticism is part of the expectation. **Sure, we can all improve our craft, but let's not harmfully judge our works in progress while we're still trying to create them.**

- **Just keep working**. Don't drive yourself kooky with navel-gazing and nit-picking apart your latest pieces. **Set a timer as you sit down to work and don't scroll back in your camera roll or your latest written draft until the timer dings.** I have a very low-fi kitchen timer that I bought for $5 at the local grocery chain a few years ago that I use for free-writes and photo shoots. The most it will offer is fifty-nine minutes, but that's more than enough time. I set it for forty-five to fifty-five minutes at a clip and, until the ding has dung, no peeking, just progressing! (How low-fi is it? I'll tell you how low-fi it is: there's no battery; it's a hand-wound timer! Each satisfying little bend-back of the dial sets the stage for an outpouring of creativity with each click-click-click. Frequently, I get so engrossed in whatever I'm making that the bell gives me a little jolt. I wind 'er up for forty-five more and back I go.) In fact, I recently started a photography series of everyday objects that have great meaning in my life, and I had a shoot *starting* the timer itself. Phone timers will also work (although you don't get that satisfying, so-last-century wind-up motion). (Check out the PDF photo file at melaniedfaith.com/photography-for-writers for a peek at my timer in photos #5 and #6, which I photographed as part of my Artifact Series of everyday objects which have great meaning in my life.)

- Remind your inner critic at regular intervals: **Making is your birthright and life's work. Creation is innate, spontaneous, mysterious, raw, unfiltered, and fun. You wouldn't interrupt a doctor in the middle of surgery; your creating is just as important and deserves that level of respect for the process.**

Try this Prompt! Go ahead. Set your timer for forty-five or fifty-five minutes. Click or type away without stopping— no pauses for second-guessing or nit-picking. Bet you can't NOT set the timer for forty-five or fifty-five more after that. Go!

Going Incognito: Street Photography and You

I adore shoes and have a closet full of them. But not just any shoes: mostly flats. Ballet flats, brown boots with chunky soles, brogues, driving shoes, flip-flops with polka dots and sandals with faux-leather straps in confetti-bright colors, snazzy sneakers with gray ribbons or hot-pink neon laces, you name it.

This fact wouldn't be so remarkable perhaps, except rounding up to 5'2", I'm short (or, that prettier word: *petite;* everything sounds better *en français, n'est-ce pas?*). I can count the number of times I've worn a heel higher than two or three inches (or anything close) on my hands—the happiest occasion: my sister's wedding over fourteen years ago. My six-foot, slender younger sister calls me *wee one*. Conventional wisdom says her willowy figure should sport the flats and I should stride forth on spike heels, and yet, we happily favor the opposite—one of many reasons we're so amicable as siblings.

Sure, there are times when I'd love to be able to reach things (anything!) on what others consider eye-level shelves, but many other times, there are advantages to wearing flat-soled shoes. Ease of movement is one of them. I glide and go, compared to when I'm wobbling to-and-fro in taller heels. Most flat shoes have softer uppers and soles, so that they very infrequently announce my impending presence down a hallway. I can enter a space before my shoes do, observing unobtrusively life happening in the midst of life without drawing attention to myself. For a writer and an artist, this is a huge gain.

I don't just love ballet flats; I love the ballet of people going about their day, their usual habits, without artifice or the pressure to perform or entertain. As soon as anybody knows someone else has entered a room, their posture and body language change. Frequently, they feel a need to make forced conversation (if in a public or workspace) or begin to fidget or get up from their seats or make (frequently dull) small talk. While perfectly normal (I do it myself), I find life much more compelling to enter quietly as cat paws, without disrupting the normal flow.

It should be noted that people-watching does *not* have the stigma as being a voyeur. A people-watcher has an open-heartedness without any leering or harmful intention. **A people-watcher is innately curious about others' natural behaviors and their environment without aiming to control or dominate the scene or subject. People-watchers are not intrusive.**

Writers and photographers are frequently excellent people-watchers. We appreciate blending in and observing with a keen eye that which we cannot control and then encapsulating life in all of its breath-taking variety. American expatriate writers like Ernest Hemingway, Gertrude Stein, and F. Scott Fitzgerald made penning from a café table not only *de rigeur* writing practice but cool.

Street photographers are people-watching pros whose very goal is to take candid shots of others going about their regular, uninterrupted routines. Perhaps best-known (especially in recent years) is Vivian Maier. Maier was born in the 1920s and worked as a nanny for approximately forty years. During that time, and unknown to most of her employers and charges, she had a somewhat-secret life documenting neighbor-hoods in her solo travels through Chicago. What most strikes the observer of Maier's photos are the unedited expressions of joy, fear, desire, impassivity, confusion, and hope on the faces she passed by and, in most cases, pointed her shutter at without their even looking at her or realizing she was carrying a camera—a huge feat in the days of clunky point-and-shoot box cameras!

Selfies of Maier taken against plate-glass storefront windows and bounced off of other reflective surfaces show what those passersby must have seen if they noticed her at all: a modestly-garbed (often in plaid button-up shirts), middle-aged woman with dark, short hair, sometimes a hat, and a resting, somber mouth. She's certainly not someone you would take for a visionary or an avant garde artist, but that, of course, is part of the beauty—she was both, in her own pleasantly quiet way. Each shot demonstrates not only who the pass-ersby were but, perhaps more compellingly, who she must have been or longed for or found absorbing.

In a snap second while walking around the neighborhood, she spotted her subjects, slightly raised the camera, clicked, and kept walking. No time dilly-dallying. No redoes. Her judgment and framing of these shots are creative, sound, and captivating, proving her innate curiosity and talent.

Street photography is a thriving art form, especially with the advent of highly portable, excellent-quality camera phones. Maier's photos are often at hip angle (likely to conceal the camera more effectively), but no one today blinks an eyelash at a person scrolling through emails on a phone or, presumably, getting ready to take a selfie that might not be so. Ingenious, and how easy for us!

Indeed, it's refreshing to think of the non-announced photo—the tiptoe-and-gone image, composed on the run and without artifice or filter (although we certainly have the technology to filter later, should we choose). Without calling attention to ourselves and without external posing, preening, or those dreaded fish-lips and duck-faces and "I look horrible. Do-over!" **Street photography is just life in the midst of being life—with falling items, yawns, last-minute movements, slightly-blurry moving cars—and all of it imperfectly perfect.**

What skills does street photography encourage?

- **Roll with the flow of circumstances as they are.** We can't get too fussy or make story boards of our concepts ahead of time. Subjects appear for a glimmer and then keep moving—and so must we. No time to get precious about framing and focusing.

- **Practice is beautiful and necessary.** Each on-the-fly photo teaches us something that we can then apply to the next captures. As photographers, there's nothing wrong with keeping some photos unshared on social media. In fact, it's preferable in many cases until we start to see similarities in what themes begin to emerge in our street shots. Unshared photos are a part of our natural learning curve.

- **Trust your own instincts and judgment about what makes an interesting scene or subject to document.** While I adore a good class and workshop, sometimes too many opinions can cause self-doubt about the quality of our work. No matter where you live, work, or play, a myriad of worthy photographic subjects abound. Street photography is immediate and a party of one. It teaches resilience in one's own abilities and sharpens intuition.

Try this Prompt! Today, let's create Maier-style. Choose a location you've been before and know well enough to visualize before you get there and where you'll know your prime people-watching spots. Remember, you won't be intrusive; you are to observe life as it ebbs and flows. **Plan on taking three or four shots of life as it unfolds before you and your lens, without drawing attention to yourself or your camera.**

For now, don't worry about in-camera cropping, zooming, blurry backgrounds, or any fancy techniques. Spot your subject or setting—get in, get your shots, get out. On another day or week, return to your locale and take three or four more. And then another day, take three more—if you dare.

You might be surprised how secret-agency and fun such outings soon become. **Cull the best three or four images into a photo story. Write a reflective piece**

about your on-the-sly sessions, covering one or more of the following reflections:

- What worked well?

- What made you edgy?

- What were you thinking before and after you took each shot?

- Why do you think this locale and these subjects called out to you (whether they are buildings, animals, people, or something else entirely)?

- Why are these three or four your favorites?

- What do they suggest about your tastes as a maker and you as a person?

Bonus, Related Prompt! Sometimes, street artists combine three or more connected photos into a narrative. Street art can be effective social commentary. Maybe your story shows a run-down house, neighborhood, or abandoned community garden that could use some volunteers, funding, and effort to rebuild. What do your photos show about both the opportunity and the challenges that exist side-by-side in this place? Maybe your story could shine a light and motivate willing volunteers. Motivating community involvement and compassion are yet other possibilities to explore with street photography.

The Extraordinary Ordinary: Finding Your Subject Just Around the Corner

"I TAKE PHOTOGRAPHS IN MY NEIGHBORHOOD. I THINK THAT MYSTERIOUS THINGS HAPPEN IN FAMILIAR PLACES. WE DON'T ALWAYS NEED TO RUN TO THE OTHER END OF THE WORLD." —SAUL LEITER

I climbed into the shower today. After having first washed my hair, scrubbed, dried off, and dressed, I then climbed back in. With shoes. And a camera.

Why did I do this? You ask. As I was getting ready to step out of the shower a few minutes earlier, I noticed the glimmering drops of water on the shower-curtain liner. It was an overcast morning, with a diffuse light from the tiny window. Normally, morning sun pours through that window, but today, the muted light showed off the drop-lets in a pattern that I'd previously overlooked. The new shower curtain liner has been up for months and months, and I never before even gave it a thought that the water pattern would make a compelling composition.

You might think this is the strangest place I've gone with a camera and an idea, but nope. And I encourage you to also chase down the random, the oddball, the quirky and even the down-right ordinary in out-of-the-way places when you get that crazy little "hmm … that's kind of cool at that angle" feeling.

Could there be a more basic subject than water? Small, little drops of agua? Collected on, of all things, an under-$5 plastic shower liner—something most people would agree is very utilitarian and useful, but not so big on glamor or remarkable qualities. And yet …

And yet, it tugged at me as having inherent possibility. It resonated in that moment as something that I might highlight and play with, both in the way I photographed it (the angle, close-up, with the drops in foreground and the soft, diffuse window light in the background, to name a few in-camera choices) and with software filters post click. (Check out the PDF photo file at melaniedfaith.com/photography-for-writers for photos #7, #8, and #9.)

No subject is too simple. Seen it a hundred, or even a thousand times? Ditto. How many times do you think I've pulled back that shower-curtain liner and never given it a second thought?

If it resonates, even just for a moment, and you pause to notice it, it's calling to you. Give it a shot, pun intended. Snap a few. The worst that can happen? You have a few shots you'll take and play around with later and possibly show no one. No harm done. Think of it as practice.

Best-case scenario, and what happens more often than not: you load the photos and discover there's something there worth exploring further; you were right.

- **Trust your gut instinct.** Our subconscious stores so many of our memories and life experiences, and it's this same subconscious that we can rely on artistically to give us that little "hmmm …" feeling when a new (or a seen-a-hundred-times) subject is near. Don't question it. Follow it.

- **Remember: wonderful photos can be made from literally any subject, big, small, or smallest.** Even household objects—an alarm clock, a pillow, a tray, teaspoons, a shower-curtain liner (Ahem! I've photographed all of these)—can make intriguing photos if you apply your own style and panache to both the way you take the shot and the way you post-produce it.

- While it's awesome to travel to exotic locales or historical hot-spots to photograph the one-of-the-kind and the monumental in scale and the rare (Bonjour, la Tour Eiffel! Hello, Taj Mahal!), that kind of experience is pretty rare for most of us. More often than not, we're going to be surrounded by signs of our everyday lives, and there's nothing wrong with that. **In fact, it's probably easier to express your own individualistic vision in home surroundings than it would be to be the billionth person to take a photo of the Leaning Tower of Pisa.** There's certainly nothing wrong with trips, and I do love me some travel photography (haven't seen the Eiffel Tower yet, but I have a few shots of the Tower in Pisa where I pretend to hold up the sagging monument—

really original, I know). Still, most of our really innovative photographs—the ones that make us grow as artists and test our skills the most—will be shots taken in or near our homes and home communities. Believe it or not, you probably have enough material in your home, even if it's a studio apartment, for a lifetime of photos. We don't always have to move onto a new subject.

- **KISS. When I was in a youth group years ago and we planned outings and fundraisers, one of our adult leaders used to repeat this mantra. It's not super flattering, but it applies in many life situations: keep it simple, stupid.** A lot of surprisingly resonant art has grown out of basic, even mundane, subject matter. The more complex or complicated the shoot or the subject matter, the more there is to juggle in the composition. Choose one theme, one idea, or one subject and make that subject unique in some way. Maybe you zoom in on the braided trim of a throw pillow and blur the rest in the background so that it's not immediately recognizable as a pillow. Highlighting smaller details of a whole object is just one of many ways to make viewers take notice of a new aspect of something they're used to seeing. Or, as Coco Chanel, the designer, used to say: "Simplicity is the keynote of all true elegance."

- It doesn't matter if other people immediately "get" why you want to photograph this theme or subject. You don't have to get the approval or go-ahead of your social-media followers before or even after a shoot. **It doesn't matter if others will or won't consider the subject "art" or not. If it resonates to you, then anything is worthy of documenting on film. Go ahead!**

• **Just because a subject has been covered before, many times (water, anyone?), doesn't mean you shouldn't. In fact, you definitely *should*.** Each artist brings their own spin and their own myriad choices in-camera and post-production. There are billions of water droplet photos, but you'll make your own distinctive ones. I did.

Try this
Prompt! Take a water photo. No, you don't have to climb back into the shower (unless you want to). The neighborhood pool, a birdbath in the backyard, the middle of a crowded city street with rain plinking off of a passersby's hair, a tumbler of water on a card table, you name it. Stretch your imagination to include the marvelously mundane. Go!

Imagery Inventory

Finding Your Imagery Style: Discovering Patterns that Excite You

Answer these focused questions to begin exploring what images resonate with you and to stir your artistic process. There are no right-or-wrong answers, and all questions are guidelines as you discover your natural tastes and develop them further or try new ideas. Enjoy!

- Name two or three colors you consider your favorite. Describe how these hues make you feel. The more specific the merrier. Instead of blue, list the shade: indigo or sky blue, for instance.

- Now, list a color you detest and why. What does that shade remind you of?

- Take two photos—one with your favorite color and one with your least-favorite hue. How do you feel about both photos? Compare and contrast. Write for five minutes. Go!

- List one or two shapes you are drawn to, whether in your photography or in your surroundings/office/room/apartment or house. What is it about the shape that feels intriguing or satisfying to you? What about textures—do you prefer hard or scratchy textures to soft or furry ones? For example, here's what I wrote for one of my shape preferences: *I tend to gravitate to threes. They don't have to be in triangles, but they can be just as satisfying side-by-side. Many of my poetic stanzas have three lines. On my desk, I have three cups of pencils and pens in a row. Threes feel interesting to me because they are not pairs—evens—but instead, have an additional element to offset the other two elements. That unevenness sheds light on the differences and similarities of each part.*

- If you had to pick one of the following to describe and/or take a photo of, which would you choose: pets, people, inanimate objects, or plants/vegetation. Why? What fascinates you about this category of images? What in your past inspired this interest?

- When you take photos, what is your POV? For instance, do you usually have a top-looking-down vantage point? An eye-to-eye with your subject view? Or a below-looking-upward POV? What about this POV intrigues you and feels like the best way to approach your subject?

- In your compositions, do you like small objects close-up or a large scene with many details from afar? Or somewhere in-between? For instance, some writers and photographers like to show one tiny object close-up to highlight its magical qualities while other artists find that approach boring or average and instead prefer sweeping scenes with several images within a single frame. Jot a few lines about your distance preferences and why either extreme close-up, mid-level view, or landscape style appeals to you, whether it's a past experience, your birth order, or a detail about your personality and organizational likes and dislikes that influence you. Go with your gut.

- If you had to choose between a scene with bright lights, a scene with little light and some shadow, or a scene with low or ambient light, which appeals the most to you? Why?

- Are you drawn to lots of bright colors, pastels, muted tones, or variations of black and white? Rank these four options in favor of your preference. If unsure, look through your camera roll and note the option you use most. Is there an option that you haven't photographed much but which you'd like to? What do you think this other color palette would bring to your imagery?

- Let's talk about symbolism and metaphor! List two subjects you photograph and/or write about repeatedly. Describe these objects, people, or places in one hundred and fifty words. Then list two reasons why you repeatedly revisit these subjects. What about these subjects might you see from a new angle or describe with new words? What do you think these subjects symbolize in your current life or the life you'd like to live in the future? What qualities do they represent about you as an individual artist? Break out your camera and take a photo of these subjects in a way or from an angle you've never thought about before now.

- List two or three places, people, objects, or other subjects on your dream list. Why haven't you photographed these subjects yet? Now, pick one of them and write one hundred words or more about how you might create an action plan to photograph it this week. No detail is silly or too big or small. Think about light and shadow, color or black-and-white, where you'll photograph it, whether it will be from close-up or far-away, and any other details you'd like to consider.

- How much blank space (empty areas on the periphery OR empty areas not related to your subject directly) is in your photos, if any? How would you feel about including more blank space in your images? What might it bring to your images to include some blank space? What might it detract from? What's one item you can crop/cut out of your image? A good way to approach this question is to take a photo with some blank space near your subject. Try another photo with no blank space surrounding your subject. Compare and contrast. Go!

- If you had to choose between plain, mildly patterned, or highly patterned, you would choose which one? Why?

- Which feels more comfortable to you: soft-focus or sharp-focus imagery? List several adjectives that describe soft-focus images. Then, list several adjectives to describe sharp-focus ones.

- Pick three adjectives to describe what you've learned about your imagery style so far and briefly explain/write impressions. For example, mine are: *vintage, imaginative, and gamine. Vintage* because I am drawn to basic items from the past, especially from the '40s-'60s; I like authentic subjects with history or backstory to them. *Imaginative* because I like brightness, primary colors, and flights of fancy in imagery. *Gamine* because my style is feminine and resonant, yet with a touch playful.

- For the time being, forget limitations of time, money, and shyness/decorum! If conditions were ideal, what ideas would you pursue in imagery? What about that imagery appeals to you? Get as descriptive as you'd like. What would it feel like to take a photo of that subject and delve into the idea with your camera and, later, your pen? Jot questions you have and would like to explore about this subject. What scares you a little about making this image? If you could take one step this week towards exploring this ideal image and getting past your comfort zone, what would it be?

Big Value, Small Consistent Investments: On Artistic Challenges

Here's a handy-dandy daily prompt list to take for a spin. I often advocate to the students in both my writing and photography classes the benefits of taking a daily, weekly, or monthly challenge.

It's stunning the creativity that results from consistent practice, and certainly I'm also a fan of prompts. I've taken both daily-for-a-month and weekly writing and photographic challenges, and at the end of each challenge, I'm happily amazed by the sheer amount of new work I've created that I likely wouldn't have otherwise.

I've prepared this list for you, but there are numerous ways you can explore a daily challenge. I'll list a few ideas that student photographers and writers have told me worked well for them; adopt the methods that make sense for you and your writing practice.

- To get into the practice of awakening your Muse, **pick a time of day (morning, noon, night) and**

an hour, and take the prompt for a spin at the same time every day. Within a week or so, you'll likely begin getting two or three possible ideas for each prompt.

- **Begin each photography session with a free-write on the theme of the day. Then, take your camera outside or around your abode to capture a coordinating photo.** Photography can enhance poetry and prose, and vice versa. Why not combine your two artistic loves?

- **Recruit a friend.** Agree to meet once a week to share the seven photos you've created from the prompts that week. You may want to meet up at a local café or restaurant to chat about the prompts that were easiest, hardest, or most surprising during your creative process that week. If you live far apart, no problem—that's why Skype, email, and texting exist; virtually meet up for a few minutes or a half hour and swap images and encouragement.

- **Lunch break-a-palooza!** Take your phone or digital camera with you on a fifteen- or twenty-minute walk during your break. Challenge yourself to take two or three (or more) shots that fulfill the daily prompt. Most of the prompts I've chosen are broad enough that there could be endless possibilities for each word. Choose your favorite shot later.

- **Gather a group of buddies and agree to each write a list of thirty-one prompts. Swap lists** with someone else in the group. A month later, host or organize a potluck. Bring your top three favorite photos from the month and get ready to share your process entailed and delicious goodies with your group. Optional: prepare a written paragraph or two before your potluck about what both challenged and happily surprised you about any of the photos you've chosen. **This idea would also work well with the recruited friend listed above.**

- **Pick your own topic and combine with the list into a project.** Always wanted to create a photobook? Have a favorite theme or motif you enjoy photographing, from landscapes to still-life images to figure studies to … just about anything, really? **Why not use the prompt list below to take thirty-one different photos of the same or a similar subject? At the end of the challenge, choose your top fifteen or twenty shots to compile into a book. Add more and expand beyond the challenge photos later.**

- **Aim for a photo each day for a month, but what if you don't have that much creative time? No problem.** Try taking two or three prompts for a spin per week or taking one prompt for a spin on the same day for four weeks. I've also had students who enjoyed picking their favorite seven from the list and taking photos on those seven prompts (in any order) each day for a week. Make a combination from the prompt list and a number of days in any way that will work for your schedule.

Insert your own idea of how to use this prompt list here:

Without further ado (drumroll, please!), the prompts:

Day 1: Red
Day 2: Tender
Day 3: Shoe
Day 4: Purple
Day 5: Tree
Day 6: Morning
Day 7: Contrast
Day 8: Hat
Day 9: Path
Day 10: Cold
Day 11: A Pair or Duo
Day 12: Multi-color
Day 13: Reveal
Day 14: Triangle
Day 15: Reflection/Reflect
Day 16: Yellow
Day 17: Bed
Day 18: Zig-Zag or Pattern
Day 19: Shadow
Day 20: Escape
Day 21: Light
Day 22: Fresh or Green

Day 23: Brown or Waterproof
Day 24: Cozy
Day 25: Black
Day 26: Shiny or Playful
Day 27: Sign or Blue
Day 28: Obstruction or Floral
Day 29: Time
Day 30: Water
Day 31: Orange

Try this Prompt! At the end of your challenge, take a half hour to journal about your experience.

Possible topics might include:

- Which photograph is your favorite, and which is your least favorite? Describe these photos in concrete nouns and with dynamic verbs.

- What did you learn about your image-making process?

- Make note of any funny, fun, or quirky details that took place while taking these images. Often, we think we'll remember our creation process for weeks or months, but it's seldom so. Jot down these creation memories now.

- What obstructions challenged you, and how did you work around them to establish a creativity routine?

- What subjects or themes recurred in your photography? What does that say about you or your surroundings?

- Would you have created as much imagery without the challenge in place? Why or why not? How might you make writing and/or photography a regular part of your life?

- Would you like to do another challenge in the near future? Why or why not? If yes, when might you schedule another challenge? Plan for future creativity now.

- Craft your own prompt list. Take the list for a spin and/or trade with a friend to double the fun.

Section Two: Practical Craft Tips and Topics— The Intersection of Writing and Photography

The One with a Science Fair in It

Last week, one of my favorite seniors invited me to her science fair. I'm not very tech-savvy and anything beyond basic accounting gives me hives, but when a student you've worked with for four years personally e-vites you, it's an honor and you go. How glad I am that I did. Science fairs ain't what they used to be!

It was the first such fair I'd attended since second or third grade in the '80s, where my two-dimensional white poster board with pie charts colored with markers slightly outside of the lines was propped onto a conference table. So lo-fi and last century! These scholars blew my mind.

Set up in the window-glass-encased lobby of the campus art gallery, the students hovered near their designated projects to answer questions and demonstrate the concepts they'd explored for the past year. Combining research and initial sketches, computer programming, math equations galore, and creative vision, their projects covered a wide array of ideas. A sampling of their projects:

- A 3D-printer-based project that crafted stackable plastic animals and a clickable pen (much like a fidget spinner) for students with ADHD, complete with the printer set-up to demonstrate and a PowerPoint of the steps taken to draw, mathematically calculate, and craft these cuddly plastic designs I dubbed "dippos" (dog-faced hippos).

- A star-shaped jewelry box with a mechanical motor that lightly tilted and spun.

- A life-size model of a studying seat on wheels (sort of like a sleek Hot Wheels meets Fred Flintstone-mobile) made of plywood and with solar panels.

- A hand-designed and hand-sewn running jacket designed for maximum velocity and including a whisper-light heart monitor.

- A self-watering hydroponic garden in a moveable cart

- The three-foot, working model airplane with neon purple and pink wrap on the wings to enable it to fly more aerodynamically (alas, they were not allowed to demonstrate flight in the glass gallery, but how delighted the pair was to explain their crafting process as well as the ice-scraper-crossed-with-cigarette-lighter thingamabob that had melted the tape onto the plane wings!).

- A trellis that cleaned and reused fish-tank waste to fertilize tiny plants

- A hand-made telescope

- A four-foot model tank submerged in a tub of water. There were two circular pieces fit into the tank that spun and ran it back and forth in the tub. The creator explained that, just two weeks before, he'd forgotten to replace the cardboard parts with plastic ones and had melted components after the initial water-dunk testing that he had to replace.

One of the most interesting parts of the science fair for me: hearing the students explain to friends, faculty, and family their process of intellectual trial-and-error while exploring initial hypotheses. There was a lot of problem solving going on!

These high-school seniors stunned with their poise, vision, and math and engineering prowess, not to mention their carpentry and spatial skills. One of my favorite questions to ask the inventors was: "What inspired your idea for this project?"

From their answers, I kept thinking that engineering and science problem-solving shares a lot in common with photographic problem-solving. Student after student explained seemingly tiny setbacks that created the need to shift perspective and try another option (often several options) for reaching their goals.

Much like photographers and writers, the students spent a year on their projects exploring not only *What is this thing I want to share and how can I craft it?,* but just as importantly, considering issues like budget constraints, the outer reaches of what software could do, and deadlines, *How can I make the most out of my creative limitations?* Students were graded based on their finished product as well as a written paper outlining their analysis of the making process—from initial idea, research, explaining setbacks and "fixes," to the final reflection of what they'd do differently and what they've learned from their project.

Creative limitations abound. As high-tech as our digital cameras, cell phone cameras, printers, and software have become, **photography is an art that similarly requires patience, do-overs, and practical adjustments over and over.** Among them:

- Low light

- Extreme light that causes dodges and burns in the image.

- Cluttered backgrounds with unwanted elements. I can't tell you the number of times I totally miss an unwanted object or person lingering in the background until I've loaded the image on a bigger computer screen and it's too late.

- Action shots where the shutter closes too early or too late and the desired moment is missed entirely. When my darling nieces were toddlers, I often just missed their adorable smiles but landed instead on puzzled or quizzical expressions, or when I asked them to hold still for another second but they zoomed out of the frame so that only a stray curl, arm, or sneaker ended up in the image. I've also worked around being a passenger in a car while spotting the perfect landscape image that otherwise would have disappeared in a flash if I hadn't raised my camera in that moment. (Check out the PDF photo file at melaniedfaith.com/photography-for-writers for photo #10.)

- Undesirable weather conditions (here's looking at you, unexpected downpour).

- Time restrictions—from taking photos with the window down from the passenger side of a moving vehicle (I've done this on more than one occasion) to taking photos of objects that have a short shelf life. Ever try taking a photo of a bowl of soup that started with that curlicue of captivating steam that descends at warp speed to a frigid bowl of broth with that kind of scum that grows while fiddling with F-stops and other dials? Yep, totally happened. Wilty lettuce is a real pain, too.

These are just a few examples; I'm sure you've encountered more (me, too). **All of these problems, though, provide opportunities for unique fixes.** For instance, I've often taken photos of the same item or event numerous times and from various angles (high, medium, below, beside, afar) knowing that I probably won't notice the obstruction lurking in some of them until I've screen-loaded them later. For low light, many photographers carry a cheap, collapsible reflecting disk (sometimes sold for under $20 online). Other photographers place their subjects closer to the window (even easier). While I can't control the weather yet (insert mad-scientist cackle here), I've started to plan better for food shots and time-sensitive ideas. Sketching some ideas, envisioning placement of the flat lay (from plate to silverware to everything else in the shot), and taking some test shots while experimenting with f-stops long before a morsel of hot food hits the plate, are all techniques to cut down on guess work and technological fumbling while the fruits turn brown and limpid foods stale-ify.

Just like my student's science projects, for every limitation encountered, there are possibilities for corrections and the potentiality for even-better outcomes than originally envisioned. **Every single photo doesn't have to be shareable or publishable. Some photos teach us and are important trial-and-error steps to future, more-focused images. Take the pressure off, and learn from each shot, especially those quirky, problematic ones.**

Try this Prompt! Reflect on a recent photo or photo shoot. What limitations did you encounter? What one action step could you take the next time you photograph this person, place, item, or event to work around the snafu you didn't see coming this time?

Bonus points for getting out and about with your camera today and re-shooting that photo (with or without the same circumstances or original location). The more we practice our craft, the more we're ready for whatever the actual photo shoot dishes out.

Ah ... Sweet Silence! Crafting in the Calm

I am a fan of hushed public spaces that have held—or soon will hold—groups or crowds. That's right—the vacancy. Many people might like the *during* experience of an auditorium or classroom and to a certain extent, I do; but as an introvert, I prefer the *just-before* or (especially) the *just-after* when the energy of the presentation/performance and so many different ideas shimmer in the emptied space. The ebbing of so many struggling, anticipating minds.

At one of my jobs, I tutor high-school students on an elegant, Gothic-looking prep-school campus. One of my favorite workdays is late Sunday afternoon. Why? The academic building where I work is always nearly empty during that time. After the satisfying little click of my key in the door of the third-floor corridor's far end, I prop open the office door with a pile of outdated chemistry textbooks and enter into a placid space that usually buzzes with teens typing away at homework assignments, searching for sources, and wrangling misshapen Frankensteinian thesis statements.

On Sundays, the white-board-topped desks with their jars of markers beckon the brainstorming ahead. On Sundays, students enter one by one in concentration for the week before them. There's little weekday shoving and yelling down the descending stairwells, no rush to get to class before late bell, no get-away-as-fast-as-we-can. Even the sunlight seems to filter through the two embankments of South-facing windows with a chill charm.

While I enjoy plays (I've lost count of the number of summer stock theater plays and the many excellently rendered student productions I've attended), concerts, and baseball games, to be truthful, my favorite moments in public spaces are when the quiet takes over—it's when I think most clearly and linger longer in the possibility of the place and my surroundings.

There's a stereotype that to create moving, relevant art, we makers should be in a near-constant state of euphoria and frenzy. That we must live our lives on the very edge of collapse to create anything interesting enough to share. That the minutiae of everyday life can't possibly be a suitable subject for writing or photography.

That's certainly not the way I make my best art, how about you?

When we are in the midst of hubbub and crisis, we often react and rush forward, rather than interacting with curiosity. When we are in the middle of dissension, it's difficult for the small voice within to have the space and freedom to play unhindered.

When we are unruffled and lull the pace a bit,

however, the eyes begin to see with new potential. The way the sunlight hits the metallic arc of the door-frame and creates a mini prism in the air. The jewel-toned tips of the markers in emerald, raspberry, and persimmon hues. The sprightly, filigree shadows the spring leaf blossoms make against the ivory wall as a breeze laces through them.

Ordinary, but extraordinary: as our artistic seeing should become. No need to be an introvert to tap into the latent possibilities in places that at first blush appear blah, boring, or overdone. True, it's virtually impossible not to live an overscheduled, next-next-next existence in these days of near-constant online interaction, and yet ... Leave even a wedge of room for the quieter, still spaces and watch what wondrous resonance appears in your art.

Try this Prompt!

Your challenge today:

photograph places that hold the suggestion of people but not the people themselves. Maybe it will be a sweater slung over a chair back. Or a slide at the park. Or an empty auditorium seat. Photograph for twenty minutes, from various angles, and then write about the experience in your writing notebook.

How is the item or place symbolic for the community it serves? What would you like a viewer to say or feel about your photos commemorating this item or place? Which photo is your favorite and why?

A fun corollary assignment: return on another day and with a different mindset to photograph the same item or place, now that you've had a chance to collect your thoughts and reflect. What remains the same about your photographic approach? What has changed?

Meet ROY G BIV

When I think about my early school years, a lot of acronyms jump out at me. From science class in elementary school: NASA (I was a child of the end-of-the-Space-Race '80s), AFS (I belonged to the international student-American student exchange organization and made friends from all over the world while in high school), and ROY G BIV from art and earth-science classes.

Yep, out of all of the acronyms, the latter is the one most likely to sound like a character's name.

"Did you hear what Roy G. Biv did with the rental car? Epic!"

"Roy G. Biv, step to the plate. Go on! Our team's counting on you."

"The brass sign on his desk read Roy G. Biv, attorney at law, and yet he showed up to Nell's party wearing turtle-patterned swimming trunks."

Not just a clever memory device to recall the spectrum colors (red, orange, yellow, green, blue, indigo, violet—I always forgot indigo without the acronym), ROY G BIV made me see the ordinary world around me with more-aware eyes. Just how purple was violet and how blue was indigo, anyway? What about the hues that are a blend that's almost impossible to tease out— the orange-reds, the yellow-greens? It reminds me of that meme that was popular a few years ago where some people saw the dress as white and gold and others saw it as blue and black. The SAME dress! For the record, most times my eyes saw it as white and gold, but one or two random times, it was blue and black.

Whether we shoot digital or analog, color theory can be a huge asset to the development of our work. Even if you prefer shooting in black and white (more on that art form in another chapter), understanding the interplay of dark and light shades is beneficial.

Colors have temperature. There are warm colors—red, yellow, pink, orange. There are cool colors—blue, green, gray, purple. As artists, we can play with choosing color temperatures that underscore theme, mood, and style. Repeated imagery that creates a pattern is called a *motif* in both literature and the visual arts. My students used to read an 1893-published novella called *Maggie: A Girl of the Streets*, by Realist author Stephen Crane, whose fiction focused on social issues. Red and its synonym variants, such as "crimson," recur again and again to emphasize and develop violence, illness, passion, drunkenness, and misplaced anger.

In our photography and writing, too, we can choose a specific color to explore an idea and develop a narrative. I've been working on a series of photos, called *In the Green*, for two or three years. Green is my favorite color, and I wanted to explore all of the connotations and emotions implied by the shade. Some of the shots are ones you might expect, including nature (a grape leaf in the shape of a rounded heart), while others don't have a direct correspondence to given cultural meanings of green (such as: go, money, jealousy, and prosperity) but include personal connotations or a scrim of the shade that popped out at me as interesting (such as a green-painted upright piano I spied at a fabric emporium in the American Midwest when visiting my sister). (Check out the PDF photo file at melaniedfaith.com/photography-for-writers for photo #11.) The composition doesn't have to be awash in the color to invest meaning for the viewer.

Colors may also bring the viewer's attention to shape, form, or line in the composition. It might be that the color outlines an object or that you make decisions to crop out or zoom in to create a shape from a part or all of the subject's pattern.

Contrast is one of the best ways we can work with color to underscore meaning. Primary colors—red, yellow, and blue—and secondary colors—green, purple, and orange—can be combined in contrasting patterns to great effect. Generally, colors opposite each other on the color wheel complement each other, while combining a primary color and a secondary color creates a contrast that is compelling. Yellow and purple is one combination of contrasting colors. Orange and blue is another. Red and green is a third contrasting combination.

Color theory is direct and helpful, but it's not simplistic. As you'll note, red and green also carries cultural imagery associated with Christmas, so **keep in mind that colors (even in combination) don't always just have one (or even two) meanings, but a multitude of personal and cultural resonances.**

Calming, neutral colors include gray and brown.

Combining a bright color, such as red or orange, with a neutral, such as tan, can create a balance between energetic and soothing elements in a composition.

Along with color theory, it's good to keep in mind that photography is a medium of light. Our eyes go straight to the lightest and darkest objects within a photo. Knowing this, we can move our light source (or our subject) to highlight elements so that they grab a viewer's attention. For instance, if we're taking a portrait and want to emphasize the subject's eyes, it might be a good idea to make them the lightest or darkest/brightest part of the composition and to move the light source or the subject towards the light accordingly.

Our favorite and our least favorite colors are often a matter of highly subjective personal opinion. On one hand, we should work inherently, gravitating towards hues and shapes and subjects that speak to us as individuals. On the other hand, keep in mind that works of art, like literature, ultimately have audiences who likely have different experiences with colors and various favorites and least favorites. **Working with the color wheel and color combinations in mind helps to steer your audience directly to elements you want them to notice.**

In the end, ROY G BIV is a matter of a nice balance between personal favorites and wider symbolic meanings.

Try this Prompt! Begin a photography series with one color emphasis, like my *In the Green* series. (Check out the PDF photo file at melaniedfaith.com for photos #12 and #13.) Over the next week, take at least ten photos that include your chosen color. Compare and contrast the shots. Which ones were most successful in conveying motif and meaning? Which shot(s) could have been taken differently to highlight the hue better, and how? Reshoot the lagging shots now that you have a better game plan.

Beware the Giant Claw: The Tricky Matter of Hands

When I was a kid, a see-through vending machine at a local discount chain always intrigued me. Standing on tiptoes, you could peer into a storage box filled with small, bright stuffed toys that seemed yours for the taking. What did you have to do to get these toys? Oh, it seemed so simple! Just deposit two quarters (at the time, our weekly allowance), grab a fire-engine red Atari-like joystick, and maneuver a shiny mechanical hand down and back up again. The hand looked like a cross between a silver octopus, a jellyfish, and a wire whisk mounted on a pole. Easy-breezy, right?

Nope. It turns out there was a trick to it. Sure, it moved off to the right and the left with absolute ease. And sure, it descended with the best of them, gorgeously gravid. Its grasp was good; its grip, however, was horrid. The problem came with clasping tightly. Its thin tentacles were the equivalent of two slippery pencils, and the grasped toy ricocheted back into the pile of plush faster than a kid on a sliding board hits the sand. I lost count of the quarters that machine swallowed up; my sister won a neon-yellow smiley-face once.

By far, one of the greatest challenges I've had photographing people is the conundrum of hands. Hands naturally draw attention to themselves. They are lithe arrows announcing: "Look here! Look here!" Many forms of dance use hands to great effect; in yoga, there are mudra that makes hands look mystical and beautiful. Yet **when the hands are static, they frequently clump, cling, flatten like a pancake, or capture like a talon. Not exactly aesthetically pleasing!**

Just like the awkward vending-machine gripper, when placed willy-nilly or even when directed to "pose naturally," **hands can resemble The Giant Claw of 1950s B-movie fame. (For an eye-roll-worthy glimpse at the sci-fi film's guilty-pleasure trailer, check out: youtube.com/watch?v=hOj0nXpRqX8 .)**

Since hands draw extra attention to their placement and form, here are some tips to work with (or around) the dreaded hand problem.

- **Think about lines and extending them.** The easiest way to make hands more visually pleasing is to make them an extension of the arm. When possible, capture hands at a side-view or tilted. The pinky side of the hand is frequently more graceful then the palm or outside of the hand, which tend to expand and create a more square or rectangular shape that resembles a blob.

- Although it was a go-to for many school photographers (I recall for third-grade pictures that our hands were placed in front of us on a faux-wooden fence for some reason), **hands don't tend to look great clasped to or piled on top of each other.** Wedding photographers sometimes use this technique to showcase love and unity themes, although they tend to choose flattering angles instead of straight ahead or top-down or hyper zooms, where hands can look heavy and flat when placed together. An exception to this, and one way to create natural symbolism, is to pair the hands with another image, such as in a diptych image where two photos are fused, side-by-side, into one panel/file. For a photo series, I merged and juxtaposed a photo I took of my parents—who have been together for almost fifty years—holding hands with a landscape photograph of two entwined trees. Entitled "Grown Together 2," the finished image symbolizes many ideas, including unity, time's swift passage, and collective identity, and *Sum Journal* published it as part of their Dyad theme about doubles. (Check out the PDF photo file at melaniedfaith. com/photography-for-writers for photo #14.)

- **Fingers create their own conundrums.** Extending fingers apart or separately in a shot can elongate them, but that can sometimes create other problems: gestures can quickly become rude or hokey, and then there's also the impolite matter of looking like they are pointing, poking, or probing. Splayed fingers can look okay (perhaps you're taking a close-up of a special ring) or they can look strange—proceed with caution. Give it a test shot or three, and then take other shots using the pinky-side of the hand to compare and contrast later. Full disclosure: I love my hands—they are small, slender, and have pretty nails that I enjoy polishing; nonetheless, I can't tell you the number of times I've zoomed in for a close-up of my hands and later noticed that my fingers looked weirdly curved or creased from sun exposure, or (gulp!) *where'd that vein below my knuckle come from?*, or widened against the surface of something, or that my nail polish had chips I hadn't even noticed until perusing the photos.

- **Palms and backs of hands tend to widen and flatten.** They have little movement and add weight and bulky dimension. **Make sure they are not pressed flat against a surface or figure, especially if the hands are beside something you don't want to add weight or focus to. Tilt, bend, or curve hands whenever you can.**

- **Does this image need to show hands at all? Could the hands be moved off to the side instead of on top or near something in the frame?** There are times when a hand can be used to highlight a feature (graceful collar bones) or to create other shapes in the image (a hand on the hip that pops out the elbow to create a figure-slimming triangle that the eye naturally enjoys). Many times, though, the hands can be omitted from an image to enhance another part of the scene or subject. You may zoom in to highlight another element of the subject. Or shift your position to crop it out of the frame. Or you might move the hand slightly (say, behind the hip in the above example so that the elbow's triangle and the curve of a subject's hip becomes the focal point; the hand is still there but no longer a main concern).

- **Use the hands to hold or to highlight another aspect of the photo that you want to have additional resonance or symbolism. Look, hands are problematic, but they can also be ... well, pardon the pun: handy.** Perhaps you want a close-up of a tiny trinket or flower. Rather than sitting the object on a table to create a flat-lay or capturing the flower in the midst of numerous other flowers, you might perch the item in a palm (using the skin and curve of the wrist as both subtle background and visual interest). I took photos of my nieces' hands with a fallen nest last summer that turned out so well that *And So Yeah* published them in their fifth issue *andsoyeah.com/?p=746.* Hands can be used to great effect to set items apart, adding a human touch. Never underestimate the value of the human touch. (Check out the PDF photo file at melaniedfaith.com/photography-for-writers for photo #15.)

Try this Prompt! Take three of these tips for a spin. Take at least three photos for each tip. Compare and contrast the nine (or more) photos later. Which ones do you think worked best for your own artistic goals for the images? Write about the challenges and successes of working with and/or around hands in your journal for fifteen minutes.

Fast and Fleeting: Capturing the Gone-in-a-Flash Subject

It's that time of the year: a torque-fueled season of quick closures. My university scholars just handed in their final projects three weeks ago, and my high schoolers are cramming (I mean: *studying*) for final exams and graduation within a week. The lengthening evenings have emerged complete with those crunchy-backed flying insects that seep out of who-knows-where at night, but the incessant clicking of mechanical pencils and highlighted textbook pages continue as our bloated brains bound forward. We're grabbing after trickles of time as we rocket-launch into a finale before summer camps and college visits (for my high school students), first-summer session at the university (for me and the grad-student writers), and later-summer visits and picnics with family near and far (for all of us).

It's another time of year, too. Here on the East Coast, the April tulips have come and gone with April's end.

Same deal with the daffodils and lilacs after two or three resplendent weeks, and (after a spring that rivaled the British Isles for consecutive crummy days of overcast drizzles in April to mid-May) the irises and roses are rollicking in their just-sprouted late-spring finery that will last through several months. There's one flower, in all of its frilly and fragrant pastel power, though, that is a mere blink and then mottled, spotted, and spent: the peony, otherwise known as my favorite bloom.

I spent an hour earlier today taking photos of the ethereal blossoms and another half-hour just before sunset picking a few for a table-top bouquet because the weather forecast again suggests gusts and gloom-falls of water tomorrow. If only peonies weren't so sensitive to rain! Just a few drops and the mold-brown blots mottle the petals. Then again, their sensitivity and the fact that they are painfully fleeting adds to their beauty, much like many time-sensitive subjects.

From documenting flowers and food (which has a troublesome tendency to cool and/or congeal or wilt) to weather patterns to one-of-a-kind moments (your kid just learned to swim and waves from the pool for about three seconds before diving back under water), **many subjects offer only-so-many chances to get a good image before disappearing.** Here are some tips for getting those gone-in-a-flash images on digital or film.

- **Carry your camera with you everywhere, and don't hesitate. Your inner voice recognizes its subject, often before it's convenient.** Seriously. Sounds so simple, right? Yet how often do you fumble for your camera or a lens and find that by the time you dig it out from a drawer, the desired moment has passed or the lighting is all wrong? Even if you carry your camera with you 24/7 or use your phone's camera (a great option these days with sophisticated technology rivaling any non-phone camera, pixel-for-pixel), if we debate about the inconvenience among ourselves instead of responding right away when we get that little nudge to document something, then the opportunity to document as-is is gone. We miss numerous great shots this way.

- **Wait where the action is (or soon will be).** Want a quick and easy way to increase the odds of a remarkable image? **Arrive early and wait with full attention.** Sit on the pool deck without scrolling the internet or having a chat, and you'll be surprised how the perfect swimming shot almost seems to find you. **Part of what makes this tip so hard and yet so simple is the undivided attention it requires; we're so used to multi-tasking that doing one thing at a time feels almost impossibly glacial and we get fidgety. Don't succumb to the fidget; focus, focus, focus!**

- **Go in with a plan.** Just as important as saying yes to the Muse the moment the ideas appear is pre-planning. **Sometimes, we know ahead of time what we want to document and that the window to capture certain shots will be very narrow.** Take the birthday girl blowing out candles or the curlicues of steam from your favorite enchiladas. Knowing that you want a close-up of the flames on the candles as well as an over-the-shoulder view of the sizzling enchiladas will help capture the key moment. Some photographers sketch the angle and other elements of the shot they hope to capture. Sure, life sometimes doesn't line up that prettily (another person might step into your frame at the press of the shutter release), and yet jotting or sketching ideas so that you go into the shoot with your main image somewhat in mind helps to guarantee that even if you don't get 100% of the shot you envisioned, your shot will contain plenty of the elements you hoped to document.

- Hey, even with planning, our best plans can go awry and none of the shots work. **Sometimes, a do-over *is* possible.** With the enchiladas example, what if they came out of the kitchen half-cold? It's possible to re-order or re-cook the enchiladas on another day, knowing that you want to shoot them when they are fresh from the oven. Food shooting can be very finicky and inconvenient, but it often offers chances for re-dos, granted with more time, money for ingredients, and planning. **Before the re-do, to ensure a better second (or third) go-round, review the shots that went wrong and write down two or three ways to improve when you re-shoot. That little bit of extra focus and analysis will help you to problem-solve on the fly in the next shoot.**

- **No one-and-done shoots. Consider shooting many stages of an event or subject, including before-and-after shots.** Sure, exact timing is tricky, especially when we know the resonant take-away image we have in mind, but there might be beautiful and resonant pictures to be had in a montage, showing the just-before and the just-after moments. I've sometimes even snapped shots of the peonies *with* their rain-damaged mottles— as with rust, their permutations may not be what some people think of as perfection but they are no less remarkable and lovely in their own way as the lines and speckles and scars on our human skin that show we endure and even thrive. Maybe a shot of the new swimmer wrapped in a towel, grinning, still wearing the swim goggles and fist-pumping with excitement wasn't what you had in mind but turns out better and more indicative of this momentous occasion than you could have envisioned. **Stay open to visual serendipity.**

Try this Prompt! Before your next speedy subject passes you by, wait where the action is, *with undivided attention.* It will be hard; after a few minutes you'll find yourself scrolling your phone or looking off to the side. Gently rein in your attention; you've got this.

Try an additional tip from the above list once you're focused to increase the odds of a remarkable, resonant, one-of-a-kind image—whether what you had envisioned or something unexpected.

Dishing up the Delish: Food Photography Tips, Part One

Markets, Shots, and Angles

One of my favorite and most-diverse subjects to photograph is food. You don't have to be a trained chef or a gourmet or even a great cook (I'm certainly not!) to practice food photography. Do you like to eat or prepare familial favorites? Enjoy the sights, scents, and tastes of trying new dishes or exploring bistros and restaurants while traveling? Appreciate the camaraderie of a shared meal or dessert? That's more than enough!

I've had the joy of creating a series of food photographs as well as teaching a class called *Food Writing for Fun and Profit: Blogs, Restaurant Reviews, Recipes, Fiction, Memoir, and More* for a few years online at Women on Writing wow-womenonwriting.com/classroom/MelanieFaith_FoodWritingFunProfit.php. It's a great pleasure to share some tricks of the trade that have helped combine two of my favorite genres.

Speaking of genre, food photography and food writing are enormously diverse, encompassing but not limited to:

- Home-cooked specialties

- Special holiday or milestone foods related to family, culture, religion, nutrition, marriage, birthdays, and breaks from fasting

- Restaurant food and/or reviews

- Eating healthfully, dieting, fitness

- Descriptions and photos on menus

- Lifestyle photography

- Still-life

- Travel photography

- Beverages/drinks

- Cookbook or blog how-tos, including recipes and step-by-step instructions on recreating main dishes, side dishes, desserts, amuse-bouches, and other elements of a meal or snack

- The home décor industry, within blogs, magazines, guides, and more

- Social-media sharing

- Advertising copy for products related to home or professional kitchens

There are three types of food shots:

- What I call **process shots**: the step-by-step details about the dish or meal and how ingredients are combined.

- **Pre-cooking shots**: this might include individual or group elements before they are combined, such as hand-rolled pasta noodles or a bottle of olive oil with a close-up of the label or the contour of the bottle. These shots can be great still-life compositions.

- **Post-production shots**. Ever taken selfies with your plated dinner? That's one example of this type of shot. These photos showcase food right-before, during, or shortly-after eating. Yes, they're still food shots if the plates are scraped and just nibbles remain.

There are also three basic approaches to angles with food shots:

- **Overhead**: perfect for whole or partial scenes that combine many elements and create a sense of bounty and/or action in the food shot. There may be many signs of different foods, dishes, and people (such as arms and hands).

- **Straight-on**: 'Nuff said.

- ¾ side view**:** particularly zoomed in to one particular element in foreground with others in the background.

Whatever cuisine is your subject, food writing and photography are big on theme and emotions, which you can tap into for the tone of the piece. You can convey such themes as comfort, community or familial connection, tradition, decadence or treating oneself, fear, body image, anxiety, sadness/loneliness, and more.

A lot of making food imagery is instinctual. "That looks amazing!" or "I miss making that with Mom!" or "That's weird/gross/yucky!"

Here are some elements I incorporate into my visual imagery to highlight the mood I'm aiming for:

- **Leave a dribble or drop as part of your styling.** While we put a lot of thought and precision into setting up a composition, as well we should, too much perfection and balance can create a ho-hum photo. To add warmth and slight imperfection to a shot, leave a drop on a cup or plate, a drip from melting food or soluble food like soup, or a bite or series of crumbs from flakey or fragile food like cookies.

- **It's all about the human touch.** While close-ups or flat-lay/top-down views of tables can be great, they can also miss out on the warmth of the feasters as they enjoy the food. Include fingers, a smile, an arm with a Popsicle drip, you name it.

- **Consider the emotional wallop of colors when creating a composition.** Warm hues—yellow, orange, red—underscore energetic, often-positive emotions but might also denote anger, frustration, or heat. Cooler hues—blue, purple, green—underscore calm, coldness, or clarity. Neutrals—tan, brown, gray— may also be used to great effect as background shades or when combined with brighter or deeper colors.

- **Ship-shape. Don't forget the value of shapes.** Consider the triangles, squares, rectangles, circles, and other lines within a composition. Use leading lines to draw the eye around shapes and throughout the composition, especially if it's an overhead flat-lay. **Table runners are an easy, inexpensive way to underscore shape and color. Another tip: I often assemble props on a table by a window so that diffuse, natural light falls across the food. Experiment with the light at different times of day**—the bright, clear light of morning; the direct, sharp light of afternoon; the buttery, sepia-ish tone of late-afternoon to early evening. **Shadows, depending on the time of day and the mood of the piece, might be an intriguing accompaniment to your composition—move props as inspired and take a few extra shots to peruse and compare later.**

Try this

Prompt! Write for twenty minutes about foods that had meaning for you as a child. Then write for another twenty minutes about foods that you've prepared or enjoyed as an adult. Who were you with? What else was going on in your personal life and in the setting when these foods were prepared/plated?

Make or recreate one of these dishes and create a photo of the meal—whether as an overhead, a straight-on, or a ¾ side view. For food-shot inspiration, peruse Pinterest and Instagram. Pair your food shots with your written essay for an inspired photo essay to submit to a literary magazine.

Dishing up the Delish: Food Photography Tips, Part Two

Affordable Backdrop Ideas and Working around Challenging Foods

Many surfaces may be used for food-shot backdrops. Often, I use plain or nearly plain backdrops so that the hues and shapes and textures of the foods can pop. **Here are some unique, easy-breezy, cost-effective backdrops I've used:**

- Burlap from a roll purchased wholesale online

- Linen

- Fabric

- Tea towels

- Wrapping paper

- Brown package-wrapping paper from a roll, from a dollar store

- A small, $10 marble cutting board from a discount chain (a total find, super heavy, though!)

- A wire cookie-cooling rack with a grid pattern, also from a dollar store

- Borrowed, second-hand antique salad plates

- Wax paper

- A scratched wooden desktop

- Colored sheets of cardboard poster board, also from a dollar store

Not all foods photograph appealingly, and compositions with challenging foods should be planned ahead and combined with prettier or easier-to-capture nibbles.

It can be super helpful to work with a food stylist or assistant, both to have another pair of hands to arrange props and foods against the backdrop as well as to fetch forgotten props. Make sure to pay handsomely in contacts, recommendation letters, salary, or a delicious meal.

Here's the deal: it's possible to take realistic photos of almost any food. Still, it's best to use "problem" foods minimally. When you can't get around such foods (perhaps you've been hired by a company to photograph a specific product), at least don't combine several "problem" foods in one composition, since you want your viewers to find the cuisine appealing. **A few such subjects that have been challenging for my photo-**

graphic practice and which friends also noted gave them fits include:

- Neutral-colored foods. Some butterscotch-tan cookies I photographed looked like anemic stones on their fancy-pants china plate.

- Mushy or lumpy foods. Here's looking at you, mashed potatoes and scrambled eggs. Applesauce can also be a challenge, although its wetter consistency fares a bit better than clumpy and clotty foods, such as cottage cheese.

- White sauces. Visions of bird feces, anyone?

- Oatmeal. An easy way to break the wall of blah mush is to garnish with bright, fresh fruits like peach slices or whole blueberries.

- Meatloaf. Loaf shapes in general don't look super appealing. 'Nuff said.

- Soups (not all, for instance, chicken noodle tends to be just fine, but the ones that have brownish chunks, such as chilis or some stews, look like puke on camera)

- Rice. White rice, especially, looks like a clumpy mound on camera. Sauces and gravies only complicate the initial problem.

- Apples or other fruits that discolor quickly at room temperature

- Vegetables prone to wilting, like kale

- Hot foods that congeal or change texture with room temperature, like pudding and its famous fast-forming scum

- Cold foods that melt with room temperature, like ice pops and ice cream

When reviewing the photos you've taken, keep in mind two or three guidelines. Would you choose this food on a menu based on your photo? Would you ask for the recipe after a single bite if it was served to you?

If the answer to either is yes, great. If not, reconsider some of your composition—whether including more-appealing hues, omitting some troublesome or unappealing foods, playing up shape, texture, or (re)moving from or adding elements to the image. Zooming in or out, cropping, or even blurring to highlight a beautiful swirl of steam coming off of a dish can work wonders to food compositions that previously weren't that appealing.

Try this Prompt! Pick one of the following six prompts. Use the others for a free-write on another day.

1. Write/type your favorite recipe and take process photos. Post on your blog or write to your favorite food blog to see if you can guest-post.
2. Pitch a story about a community-food event to a local newspaper, website, or restaurant. Some colleges and universities, charities, religious groups, and volunteer groups have yearly or quarterly festivals or other food-related events that would be a perfect food topic to cover. Spaghetti dinners, a summer carnival, community-center learn-to-cook lessons, international food festivals (my alma mater used to host two of these per year, and participating in cooking and serving dishes as well as eating many new-to-me foods, such as Korean bulgogi and Australian Anzac biscuits,

was one of the highlights of my undergraduate years), you name it. Attend the event and take lots of photos. Interview a few of the participants. What brings them to the event? What is their favorite dish at the event?

3. Write a five-hundred-word article or personal essay about a food discovery you made while traveling to another country or region. Include coordinating shots of the food and/or ingredients used to make it.

4. Visit an international market or farmers market. Buy several ingredients you've never cooked with before, which might include fresh vegetables and fruits, grains, spices, you name it. Read up on recipes that include this food or spice; give one a try. Write about your experience afterwards.

5. Write a poem or a short story about a food unique to your family, hometown, or culture. What makes this food special?

6. Write a restaurant review of a new or new-to-you place. Consider pitching it to your local newspaper or posting it on your own website or blog as a writing sample/clip of your skills and food connoisseurship.

#bwphotochallenge: Put on your Monochrome Goggles

I don't know where they came from (a dollar grab-bag from the card store? maybe a cousin's birthday party?) or how long we had them (a few months? a year?) or why there was only one pair between my sister and me, but I remember they were yellow and they were a hot commodity we took turns wearing.

The glasses had yellow frames and yellow lenses, but time could be playing tricks on my memory; the frames might have been black.

The lenses were *definitely* yellow. Canary-feathers yellow. Homemade-lemonade-in-a-glass-pitcher yellow. Sunny-Saturday-in-the-park-in-July yellow.

Slipping them on, the world turned from Technicolor to something other.

Why in the world, you might wonder, am I mentioning color in a chapter supposedly about black-and-white?

The lenses acted as a filter. They filtered out the multi-tudinous splashes of every hue under the rainbow and, in its place, drenches of yellow overtook everything. They created a uniform-ish world where the shapes and textures of furniture, clothes, lawn, and sky were the real differentiating features of people and objects, not color.

Black-and-white photography has a way of cutting out all of the visual distractions and clutter of color and creating a sleek emphasis on form, shape, and line. Suddenly, the rectangles and polka-dots and squiggly lines of patterns are highlighted. In a flash, the contrast between dark earth and light sunset is stunning. Right away, the shimmering sequins on a dress or veil dazzle with their mirroring effect.

Black-and-white photography also underscores a timeless mood that is great for celebratory photos, such as a child's first birthday, baby's first steps, a wedding, an anniversary, or a graduation. Some photographers shoot monochrome in-camera. Others use filters or software, such as Photoshop, to get a black-and-white effect from color shots. While there is some debate about this within the photographic community, whether originally a color file or negative or shot in camera as black-and-white, **monochromatic photography is its own art form that is readily appreciated. It has a wide audience, including just about any subject matter you can imagine, from landscape to human-interest to sports photography to senior portraits to architecture and pet photography.**

There are black-and-white photography contests

and exhibits. **There are also classes specifically for exploring this art form in depth**, online at Creative-Live creativelive.com as well as offline at universities and community colleges near you. **Some literary magazines I've submitted to request only black-and-white photos in their art guidelines. I've also seen and posted in black-and-white photo groups online**, such as at Instagram at #bwphoto, #bnwzone, #bwphotochallenge, #noiretblanc and #noiretblancphotographie. These online groups are also great sources of ideas for future black-and-white shoots, as well as to see how individual style, shooting angle(s), and placement of light sources affect a composition.

Libraries and Amazon are excellent purveyors of black-and-white photography books of master photographers, such as Imogen Cunningham, Diane Arbus, Paul Strand, Sally Mann, Elliott Erwitt, Edward Weston, Dorothea Lange, Ansel Adams, Henri Cartier-Bresson, Alfred Stieglitz, Herb Ritts, Malick Sidibé, Man Ray, Andre de Dienes, Walker Evans, Robert Mapplethorpe, and more. **Borrow or buy collections of work by these or other photographers to study a variety of subjects, lighting, angles, and other techniques that enhance compositions within monochromatic photography.**

Years ago, when Borders bookseller was still around (RIP, dear one), I used to peruse a fantastic, long-published magazine for artistic black-and-white photography, called *B & W (Black & White)*. A few months year ago, I became curious about if they were still publishing and, huzzah and fantastic news, they are. Better than that, they have some content from the magazine online, including select galleries as well as contests. I treated myself to a year's subscription on the spot (bandwmag. com). The print edition includes fascinating spotlight articles and interviews with top photographers. If you're interested in the potential of black and white, consider it an investment in your artistic education to peruse the website and/or subscribe. A long-published quarterly favorite out of Minnesota, *SHOTS Magazine,* also publishes beautiful and evocative fine-arts images in black-and-white and accepts submissions within the genre (shotsmag.com).

Keep in mind that many photographers who routinely shoot in color sometimes dabble in black-and-white photography, and vice-versa. It doesn't have to be an exclusive, all-or-nothing practice. **To determine if your subject might be a good fit for a monochromatic treatment, keep these guidelines in mind:**

- Is there an interesting pattern or geometrical design in this scene or in this subject?

- Does the subject or scene include interesting textures or a juxtaposition of textures that black and white might highlight?

- Is there something plain or without pattern nearby that might pair well to bring out the design or texture of this other subject?

- Is this a scene or moment where the drama of black and white could create a timeless mood?

Try this Prompt! Now that you know a few strengths of b&w photography, make a list of three or four subjects in your home, office, campus, community or region that would make great black-and-white photo subjects. After asking the above four questions, pick one subject and jot notes about the patterns, scenes, juxtapositions, light sources, angles (front or side, high, eye-level, or low, etc.), and any other ideas you have for shots. Then have a black-and-white-photo shoot.

Whether you shoot black and white in camera or add it in post-production using photo software is your choice. Shoot as many photos as you like (I often shoot way more than forty at a time), aiming for at least three to five shots from the shoot that you might submit as a photo series to a literary magazine, post on Instagram, or upload on your personal website as samples of your work.

Fascinators and Carriages: Documenting Special Occasions

"Americans are very conservative with their hats," says the broadcaster in a posh British accent.

This isn't the usual programming I wake to for my morning bathroom call at 4:30. But then this is no ordinary day: Prince Harry and American actress Meghan Markle are tying the knot. The fanfare and hoopla are at high voltage, not only in the crowds wearing their fantastic finery and waving the Union Jack outside St. George's Chapel but all over the world, courtesy of online and offline media.

I've attended many weddings in my lifetime. Pardon me if the ceremony doesn't exactly light my fire anymore. In addition to numerous friends' and coworkers' weddings, I have over thirty first cousins and I've lost count of how many second and third cousins, so you can imagine; sure, not all of us married, but some of us married more than once. No offense to anyone who grew up dreaming of the fairytale ceremony and the blow-out-bash after-party, but that's just not me.

On the other hand, I can be as girly-girl as anybody and, frankly, the coverage before the nuptials snags my attention for a good two hours. Regrettably or not, I fall back asleep at 6:15 a.m. and snooze through all of the I-dos, special music, the procession, and Princess Charlotte's cute wave as the carriage churns the newly-weds through the hysterically pumped crowds. (No worries—thanks to the internet, I miss not a jot on replay.)

That's right: my favorite part of this whole spectacle is the pre-show. The chats with military experts about Prince Harry's ten years of service in the Army. The chewing-of-the-fat with fashion experts churning rumors and mystery about Meghan's dress and if she's chosen a British designer (she did, from the French fashion house, Givenchy), the juicy dish about dress code for such an event (in case you're wondering: "day dress and hats" for women, knee-length or longer, sleeved preferably, but showing some arm won't get you kicked out, and "military regalia" or "mourning suit and top hat acceptable" for men, although there's a shocking lack of top hat, thankfully and respectfully for the people in the back pews).

I also dig the interviewing of charity-heads who work first-hand with the Prince and his brother on charities in the UK and abroad, as well as children involved with the Prince's pet charities (including, much like his mother, the AIDS crisis in Africa as well as children's cancer), experts about Meghan's role as a biracial royal as well as the numerous charities, including her work as a global ambassador for World Vision children's charity, for which she has leant her celebrity to support. There's an interview with a nine-year-old boy with a giant daisy boutonniere who cracks me up. These aspects of Harry's and Meghan's lives seem more indicative of their personalities than the pomp and circumstance, which feels very much like a made-for-TV movie. Then again, it's good fun to get lost in a movie scene now and again.

Once the doors to St. George's Chapel swung open (displaying a gorgeous wall of white flowers and a black-and-white checkered floor fit to make M.C. Escher drool), celebrities from both sides of the Pond trot down a sizeable, cobble-stone knobbed hill. One TV personality pays homage to the careful, kind way handsome George Clooney paced himself on the tricky cobblestones with mega-talented international-human-rights-lawyer wife, Amal, on his arm, looking "smashing" in "primrose yellow."

There was a lot of yellow going on. There were also some of the most fantastical, beautiful "fascinators" I've ever seen. Fuchsia feathers at space-age antennae angles, pastel pancakes like fluffy off-center berets, and breezy boater-style hats with wide brims and full-scale floral sculpture kept this event frolicsome and festive.

Oh, and the fact that the camera kept panning to two of the Prince's fully invited ex-girlfriends is an added bonus.

Royals aren't the only ones who know how to

commemorate with style. Photographers and writers alike honor graduations, anniversaries, the purchase of new homes, engagements and weddings, and a multitude of other events—from national holidays to personal achievements, such as promotions. **Some days are more special than others, and it's fitting to don some "dapper" clothes and write an ode, pen a short story, or snap some shots to record the larger-than-life (and often conflicted) emotions involved in a public party.**

The next time you are nearing a special event that begs recording, whether in photography, prose, or poetry (or, why not, all three!), here are some tips for taking your commemoration to the next (artistic) level.

- **Lead in:** Sure, everyone remembers to get the shot of the grad holding the diploma on stage or lined up with family, but what about the shot of the grad at graduation brunch before the ceremony, or putting on his cap and gown before lining up in the auditorium? These seemingly little lead-in moments tell a more fleshed-out, compelling story of the event and, long after your closest friends have posted their shots from the stage, you'll treasure the just-before rituals you captured.

- **Commemorate with special items of the time period:** When I was a senior in high school, my parents and I chose two styles of senior portraits. In one, I have the typical "fancy drape" of dark blue velvet and a stock background (also plain).

In another, I'm more relaxed, in a striped '90s-style shirt, with a journal and gold pen (props I brought myself to give a nod to my wanting to be a writer). Guess which shot is my favorite? That's right—when at all possible, personalize with objects, scenery, or props that have special meaning to the person or event.

- **It's not over until you say it's over:** Here's something I wish I'd done after my three graduations and after my sister's wedding: prepare a question or two you'd like to ask the honoree shortly after the main event. Informally seek the answer. Combine and/or store a print-out of their response(s) with copies of photos you took that day, such as in a special album online or a tactile album for your own private archives and memories of that day. This would also make an ideal gift for birthdays or anniversaries later, and a fun time-capsule (for future generations) of what you were *really* thinking and feeling on that special day.

- **Not all events are purely happy occasions**—that's cool, too. We should strive to document a range of realistic human emotion. There's a lot of social pressure with pivotal life moments and group events. Consider also exploring times of difficulty, strife, confusion, or mixed emotions. I've seen some amazing photo series made from personal struggles (such as illnesses and geographic or personal moves) that become universal in theme.

- **Don't forget you!** This one might seem self-evident, but I've heard over and over again families lament that one person was the photographer and that there aren't many pictures of this person because he or she was always behind the camera. I fully understand the impulse to stay tucked behind the camera all day (it's often more fun, especially as an introvert, and far more creative), but … don't be the ghost participant. Make sure two or three shots include you—whether selfies or via the photo skills of a fellow celebrator/guest. You may not want those photos you're in, but your friends and loved ones most likely will treasure them.

Try this Prompt! You know it's coming up—the next special event. Go ahead and jot down a question or two you'll ask following the big moment. Store the answers with eight or ten of the photos you take and get printed. Combine into a tactile album.

Whether you keep it or give it away as a gift, this treasured art form will wow 'em—if you're like me, most of your photos from the past ten years exist in the ether or on hard drives, so a real-deal album is already another cause for celebration.

The Nest: Working with Cute, Unpredictable Subjects

Call it an aha! moment. Call it my coo-coo brain that is always churning out new art projects to amuse myself. Call it photographic mayhem. Whatever you call it, the nest cooperated by falling out of the tree four days before my darling nieces arrived for a summer visit. I scoped out that the baby birds had long left their mama-made abode and were nowhere in sight; and then, I picked it up gently, cuppingly with two palms, and carried it to the porch to dry out.

As nests go, it was, indeed, a gorgeous specimen. Mama bird had spun mud in one of the most admirable concentric circles I've seen in nature (especially since it dropped the equivalent of two stories from a tree-top). Even the random too-big twigs swirled out at artful angles.

I took two or three selfies holding the nest, but the angle was contorted and who wants to see their own double-chins looking down? No, thanks. I reached for my tripod to do some razzle-dazzle magic with a timer, and then it hit me: *the nieces are coming!* Yes! I flashed to the found nest. Yes! It could be our special auntie/nieces art project. I do love me a good project.

I knew I could talk them into it. I envisioned multiple angles, laughing about the amazing lightness of the nest, tilting into and out of the sun for the best highlights of the nest, comparing and contrasting the effects of sunlight against the twigs compared to a shade-held bird abode.

Ah, yes, plans: how very quaint of me. As the saying goes: man plans, God laughs. Here's how it actually shook down:

My elder niece refused to touch the nest for about three minutes.

"It's dirty," she said.

I allowed that it did, indeed, appear dirty because of what it was made of, but actually, the inner-mud walls were already dried. I touched it to show her that holding it wasn't something to hold back from and that the nest wouldn't leave me muddy.

Cora Vi considered that thoughtfully for about three seconds. Then she nodded and asked, quietly and seriously, "Were there eggs in there?"

Always sensitive to others' feelings, this elder niece of mine—I love it, but I also wanted her to just scoop the nest into her palms and get to it in the ninety-degree heat while my makeup melted off my face. I explained that at one point, yes, there had been baby birdies once in eggs, then hatched and fed in the nest, but that the birds learned to fly and were long gone before I picked up the nest from the ground, I promised.

I assured her I wasn't a mean landlord booting hapless birdies from the nest without so much as a hobo sack.

"I triple checked that there were no birds. All gone. All big birds, after all, and flown away, just like at one point you were a baby crawling and then, *boom!*, you took off and could walk and run on your own." I said.

Then, she was willing to take the nest like a champ— for about two minutes, before she said, "I want to go inside. It's hot." My foundation half-melted like a Picasso portrait, I had to agree, and let my six-year-old niece chickadee fly back into her icy, air-conditioned inner-sanctum.

Since Cora Vi had done it, my younger niece was happy to heft the nest into the bowl of her hands held together, but she was also way more excited about poking at the little holes in the bottom with a finger. I had visions of the entire architectural marvel unraveling Three-Little-Pigs style like after the wolf huffs and puffs, crumpling the flimsy house of sticks. Uh-oh.

I fired off snaps of the shutter at rapid speed, before she chucked the nest (as three-and-a-half year-olds will do) for another amusement—a basket of shells gathered from the ocean ten years before.

- **Go in with a plan:** When working with subjects who have short attention spans or who tire easily, it's better to have your ideas for poses ready before you subject arrives. I had seen a very cool image of an artist (Cig Harvey) in a gingham dress holding an apple at her abdomen; I knew I wanted to replicate that idea but with smaller hands and torsos—and holding not fruit but a nest. I didn't explain to the girls what I was going for artistically—those details would have meant little or nothing to them. Instead, I jumped in myself and demonstrated how cool the nest was to touch. I picked up the nest in the way I wanted them to hold it and encouraged them to hold it the same. Quickly. Very quickly, transitioning between nest and camera, juggling camera and kid patience at the speed of light.

- **Stay open to serendipity:** No sooner had I passed the nest over to Cora Vi than one of the longer twigs plopped to the ground. Rather than picking it up off of the ground, we tilted the nest a bit and worked with it. With or without that tumbly twig, the photo has interest and presence. Weather conditions, movement of objects or subjects, any number of circumstances can take place to try to distract you (such as people walking by or purposely photobombing while you're trying to zero in on developing your initial idea). **Roll with the balance between what you wish for and what actually transpires.** Circumstances will rarely, if ever, be as you envisioned them, and that's just fine. Speaking of which:

- **Stay open to the suggestions your subjects offer:** After two or three shots where I demonstrated the bowl-of-hands technique I envisioned, Cora Vi said, "I can hold it this way, too." She moved her thumb a bit to the right, and I shifted my zoom so that it was a bit off-center and, according to the rule of thirds, provided additional interest. A very cool idea—and one I wouldn't have thought of if Cora Vi hadn't made her observation. You never know when your subjects will do something or say something to improve your compositions. **Be open to trying cooperative suggestions.**

- **Veer from your vision … and then back again. Adjust, adjust, adjust:** Just because your subjects aren't in a particular mood to cooperate doesn't mean all is lost in the shoot. With both nieces, there was an issue I hadn't thought of: their cartoon-character (and very copyrighted logo!) t-shirts. Oops! Thinking on my feet, I cropped in even closer than anticipated for one shot and blurred out the logo for another. Both worked just fine around the problem. To see one of the published shots from the series, "Things that Start with N—Nest and Nieces," which appeared in *And So Yeah*, visit: *andsoyeah.com/?p=746* .

- **Work faster than you think you'll need to; you'll probably need to:** I've heard pet photographers say, here one second, gone or turned or in mid-motion the next, and that's certainly held true from my own experiences trying to capture wildlife and even my darling domestic feline, Chloe. She will purr and stare right at me for minutes on end, but should I pick up the camera—well, let's just say I have a bunch of photos from the past few years of the back of her neck and the side of her ear.

- **Keep your humor:** Pets and little kids don't tend to have a lot of patience for do-overs. I could tell that both of my nieces were finished with the photo shoot quite easily—Cora Vi flat-out told me and Sylvie Ro wandered out of the frame. Both really liked the nest, although their approaches and thought processes about the nest were totally different, on-camera and off. Your subjects may have a short fuse or not take your vision as seriously (or seriously at all) as you do. **You can't control how others react or if your photo idea will bomb or fly, but you can react with equanimity. Think of your series as a grand experiment and approach with good humor.**

- **Chat 'em up:** Photo shoots and projects in general flow better when you engage with your subject directly. **Ask your subjects questions, compliment their staying style, a particular smile, or a pose they do well.** The whole time I was working with the nieces, we talked about what kind of birds we thought might have been using the nest hotel (Cora Vi thought "wobin," while Sylvie Ro, ever the blue-lover, went with "Bluebuwd"). Your subjects will relax more and feel less on-stage or spectacle-like if you make the process a positive interaction.

- **Offer rewards:** Yeah, I'll admit it. There was a little more motivation station involved. I didn't just verbally cheer them into the project; there was the promise of a nail-polish party (manicure AND pedicure) afterwards, in which we painted each nail a different color. Having snacks and/or bottled water on hand—as well as some props if you're working with young children (such as bubbles) can work well to keep the mood and the momentum flowing. Can't hurt; just saying.

Try this Prompt! If you always shoot silent or inanimate objects or flowing (mostly controllable) scenery, veer out of your comfort zone. Today you're going to shoot a series based on a loveable animate subject with its own mind, whether pet or human. Apply three or more of the above tips for your shoot. Create and add your own tips to the list as you go along and after the shoot.

Popping the Bubble: Keeping in Mind Your Subject's Needs

"Do it again! Do it again!" My nieces clapped, riveted to my face where they were staring holes into my mouth.

Of course, once they were staring this-close to my face and clapping their hands, the next bubble fizzled before it got nearly as big as the first and without the little firecracker-like pop at the end.

It didn't matter. They loved it. Feeling vaguely like a circus freak or an Instagram star, I kept at it. Bubbles — medium, small, one so large it popped beside my nose.

It never got old … for them.

My elder niece has recently been allowed to have bubblegum, but only once a day and not every day, and my younger niece has to wait for a few months.

Like cute, curious puppies, they both wanted to sniff the package. "Is that grape-flawor? Mmm."

"Smells grape! I want it! I want bubblegum."

"Sorry, honey, I don't think you're allowed yet."

"Do more bubbles!" the elder niece clamored, so the younger niece, climbing onto my torso, also clamored, "Do more bubbles! More bubbles!"

Like any good auntie … I obliged them—bubble after bubble until the gum was as tough as taffy and the resulting bubbles went from mid-size to muddling.

I'm a private person and used to a lot of personal space. While I don't mind at all to have my visiting nieces all up in my grill, it *did* get me to thinking more deeply about the ways we interact with our subjects as photographers.

Not all people want to be photographed. In a world where we can (and do) constantly update, tweet, post, and selfie, it's important to remember our desire for documentation and artistic expression doesn't always mesh with others and, in fact, might make our intimates annoyed, angry, or frustrated.

I'm as guilty of overstepping boundaries as the next person. I've stopped mid-line or mid-sidewalk interrupting foot traffic to grab a photo opp (or five).

Two days ago, I stood in line for a ride at an amusement park with the darling nieces. Seven or eight snaking rows edged forward at a snail's pace, and the grandfather and dad-to-a-toddler in front of me kept taking endless stops, holding up the line behind him, to snap away the decal illustrations on the wall filled with local history.

This is what I'm like. Yikes. I thought, biting my tongue, saying nothing as my toe tapped to get going already and a bigger gap opened up in line ahead of the forever-photo-opping family.

I fully understood their desire to document AND

how frustrating it must often be for the people behind me when I abruptly stop inches away from them—more than once. I'm usually the jerk dawdling and documenting—a good dose of my own medicine this time.

Maybe they don't want your scrutiny or attention. Perhaps any interest, despite your intentions, is too much. It's understandable—we all get days where we want to be left alone or have little patience (some of us more than others, perhaps, but all of us, still).

Respect another person's wish not to be photographed.

Apologize and move away. Immediately. Putting space between you and your not-so-happy subject can be a good idea. No shot is worth an altercation.

Don't get too hard on yourself, though. While it's not our goal to annoy or hurt others, it's also not our job to be mind-readers or anticipate everyone's reactions to what we make. Often, we don't know how others will react (especially first-time subjects) until we do, and then we can adjust (and move on) accordingly.

Try this Prompt! Write about a time when you didn't want to be documented. Include sensory images, internal dialogue, and the where, when, why, who and how details to flesh out the uncomfortable scene.

Photographing Place: Landscape and Travel Photography Tips

"PHOTOGRAPHY IS LIKE EXPLORING A NEW DIMENSION, ONLY I CAN GO THERE BUT I CAN SHOW YOU WHERE I'VE BEEN." — DESTIN SPARKS

Outside the window, there are twenty pinpricks of light on an incline, then a dip, then another bigger incline off to the right. If you squint your eyes, the lit ski-slopes look like a swimmer doing the crawl stroke—the baby slope is the side of a fine-boned face with one eye made of lights peeking above the water, while the intermediate slopes make one arm raised elegantly, arcing through the pitch-black night along rural roads without streetlights.

There are many possible approaches to documenting the geography, weather, mood, and tone of both familiar and new-to-you places. Consider these six guidelines the next time you pick up your camera to document travels near and far.

- **What distinctive features make your landscape unique? What first piques your interest about this location?** It might be as small as an abundance of ant colonies or plush grains of sand and as large as a factory or a soaring monument or a skyscraper.

- **What is the salient characteristic of this setting?** What grabs your attention and creates a sense of place?

- **Sometimes, paradoxically, the better tack to take is similarity.** How is your desert backyard symbolic for all desert backyards? What flora and fauna (or lack thereof) scream your region? What images symbolize the joys and struggles of living here?

- **What shapes or colors (or lack of color) do you notice in-camera that you can play up in your photo to create symbolism and metaphor by zooming in or cropping to enhance the shape or texture?** Take, for example, the shapes described in my ski-slope-lights example above.

- **I call this exercise "The Eyes of an Outsider." Put on your vacation goggles. What would a friend notice who has never before visited this place? Take a walk with a pal through your favorite local haunts, whether indoors or outdoors. Both of you take photos and compare what you notice in your surroundings. Then,**

each of you take photos of each other's subjects but with your own angle or spin on the subjects. Live far from your artistic friends? I feel you, and no problem. You can still do the first part of this exercise, swapping shots from your solo shoots to showcase parts of your surroundings you might never have noticed without the eyes of an outsider. Email/text your friend with reactions to their photos and note something this exercise brought out in your own photos that surprised you.

• **Take a seasonal series of the same place. Document the same subject either monthly or quarterly.** Emphasize the differing temperatures, light, clothes of passersby, growth or decline of foliage, and the like in your seasonal shots, keeping one item (a building, a mountain, a sunrise or sunset) static and unchanging in the composition. Even if you don't live in a temperate climate, the slant of light varies by season, and photography is certainly a medium that makes the most of light. Take photos of your favorite place in the rain. Take one through a window. Take one from a high angle and one from a lower angle. Mix it up, retaining just one constant element.

• **Destination Station. Drive away for an afternoon or weekend. Photograph whatever strikes your fancy in your travels.** This is a great exercise in following and sharpening your innate artistic intuition. The next week, go for a photo shoot nearer home. Seek to replicate or pair subjects in your new shots with those from your weekend jaunt. What similarities or juxtapositions might both sets of photos make? Swap with a friend, who might have new takes on the photos and how they fit together and/or develop themes.

Try this Prompt! There's no better time than the present. Set up a photo walk or a post-photo-session swap of work with a friend, and then take guidelines four or six for a spin. There's something inherently encouraging and motivating about having an artistic friend waiting for our new work; it also makes it nearly impossible to shove aside or postpone a photo shoot for errands and other life effluvia that often gets in the way of creating.

Analog-Tastic!

Thanks to the internet, people share 3.2 billion images per day on social media. That's billion, with a b, daily.

There's a whole lot of image-sharing going on (understatement alert!), and our numerous speedy technologies are making inspiration an easier and easier click of a button. **Before we get too wrapped up in the online imagery fest, however, I'd love to consider a growing type of photography that is just as inspiring and rapidly growing in popularity: analog photography.**

Analog refers to any form of camera that uses tangible film and is non-digital. As you can imagine, this includes a bevy of camera types, brands, and styles from many eras before 2000. Everything from your great-grandpa's large-format camera with the black cloth he disappeared behind to document the unsmiling relatives; to grandma's boxy Kodak Brownie from the 1950s; to the Rolleiflex with its two sleek, stacked chrome lenses that made Vivian Maier, the street photographer, famous; to your first Nikon 35-mm in college that you took into the quiet dark room to develop; to the festive Polaroid prints of the 1970s-1990s with their white-paper border that you watched develop and then sticky-tacked across your walls. Yep, all of it, so very analog.

Lomography is one of the most popular forms of

analog photography that has seen a resurgence since the Millennium. Invented in Europe (many sources say Russia and named after a popular Russian camera model from the 1980s, the Lomo LC-A), Lomographic cameras are petite, plastic, and delightfully unpredictable in the style of photos they produce. **They are sometimes referred to as toy cameras. This is no child's plaything, however, but an artistic tool that can take your Muse to new levels.**

Lomographic shots often include uneven shadowy splotches and/or light leaks that create colorful pastel splashes across the images that are, like fingerprints, utterly unique to each shot. **There's one form of Lomographic camera, a Fisheye Camera, which creates regular-sized rectangular prints, but circularly-centers subjects within the middle of the frame, just like looking into and through a fishbowl.** The edges of the prints outside of the circle are static black, and create a compelling, telescopic-like view of the world with the bends and artsy distortions from making the centered, circular image.

About fourteen years ago, I discovered Lomography and ordered a Fisheye Camera to play around with amazon.com/dp/B000JFJ06G; I took it on jaunts through the neighborhood, to a friend's birthday party, and around the office documenting the spherical curves and distortions that made each commonplace shot not only grainy by gorgeous. The edges outside of the curved central subject tend to appear darker on many fisheye shots. If you like art-house films or the intimate, lo-fi, somewhat stark but compelling look of a Polaroid print, Fisheye Lomography would be a great fit for you.

As with all analog film cameras, there's no screen in the back or erase button. You have a certain number of shots on your film roll (often twenty-four or thirty-six), some serendipity, and a shutter. It's at once whimsical and challenging.

Once you send off your film for development (or learn to develop it yourself, a handy analog skill to learn), you'll discover which shots worked, which shots flubbed, and which shots were what-in-the-world-was-*that?!*

Two other popular Lomographic cameras are the Holga and the Diana. "Dreamy" and "color-drenched" are two adjectives I've seen online again and again that describe the shots these cameras produce. The cameras themselves are petite, rectangular-ish, sometimes colorful and sometimes black, and palm-sized.

Since 1992, students in Vienna formed a worldwide club, the Lomographic Society International, for photographers who shoot using the plastic cameras of every model or make. The group operates a wonderful and informative website at lomography. com which includes sample photo shoots displayed blog-style and updated regularly for inspiration, links and content from their magazine. It also includes information about competitions, and a store where film (some cameras take one hundred and twenty medium format, others take one hundred and ten, and still others take 35mm rolls), cameras, lenses, and accessories may be purchased.

Lomography is a rich and varied source for analog techniques, but there are oodles of additional possi-

bilities since the resurgence of photo clubs and classes, both online and offline, for analog photography. You can learn how to build a pin-hole camera. You can take a class in making tintypes (similar to photos from the American Civil War) and Daguerrotypes or Wetplate Collodions, all three techniques from photography's infancy in the 1800s.

You can also learn an old-school photographic technique that (get ready for this) doesn't even USE a camera (gasp!) to create prints, called the Cyanotype. Cyan, by the way, is a color midway between blue and green on the color wheel; the resulting prints are dark blue with light-blue replicas of the subject. I first experienced making Cyanotypes (although I wouldn't know until a few years ago that they were called that) when I was visiting a State Park around age eight or nine. The park ranger and a bunch of us kids gathered pine cones, twigs, fallen star-shaped maple leaves, grass fragments, small stones, a fern frond, and flower petals and then arranged our treasures on a special kind of paper. The ranger mixed a chemical solution that was applied to the paper and left our works to dry in the dark nature center office while we went on a walk outside. We returned to the office to find magical identical imprints of our natural wonders in light blue upon a static dark blue background on the paper that we got to take home with us. Although Cyanotypes were created in 1842 by Sir John Herschel and used by engineers to make cheap copies of drawings, they are still in use today by artists.

Sure, analog photography is richly varied and includes some cool techniques but why, as a writer

and an emerging photographer very much in the twenty-first century, should you care?

- Analog Photography encourages **a slowing-down and seeing** that our digital and camera phones just cannot compete with. I cannot emphasize this enough: artistic breakthroughs most often happen when we slow down a bit and declutter. In other words, they happen when we give ourselves and our schedules a little breather, a little room to play and think instead of rushing-rushing-rushing breathlessly to the next appointment and then the next. As a freelance editor and teacher at three schools who also writes my own work, I'm as guilty of this over-scheduling as the next person. Yet really kicking back, which is what these photography techniques demand and then encourage, is where most of the magic happens in my photography and in my writing. Surrender to the technique, and the magic will follow. Tonight, to write this chapter, I momentarily threw over answering four emails and grading papers.

- **You can network with super cool people you might not meet any other way.** People interested in photography techniques are the types of crafty, intelligent, zany, amusing peeps who have other artistic interests that will broaden your own mindset and skillset. That new pal from your Ambrotype class spins wool and knits amazing toys. Your amigo in your wet-plate seminar plays bongos in a Salsa band on the weekends. As a writer, it's not just the techniques that will spark your Muse but also the stories of the people you meet who will infuse your curiosity and get the words—and images—flowing.

- Maybe you're an introvert who would rather putter around in your own backyard or office. **These photographic techniques are positively begging for introvert attention.** The details you glean through the mechanical, physical processes of analog photography encourage the kind of in-the-moment, visionary self-reliance that can only enhance art-creation. Introvert away!

- **Recognize that you are not giving up the digital forms of photography you already practice—you are adding an exploration of new methods** that will enhance the way you approach your creativity and offer new ways of slowing down so that your openness to ideas flourishes in unexpected ways. Exciting stuff!

Try this Prompt! How can you add analog photography to your image-making arsenal?

Explore the Lomography site (lomography.com) or do your own search for Lomographic images. What type of Lomography/Lomographic camera appeals to you most? Purchase a Lomographic camera (in the $40-100 range new) and take it for a spin; I bought mine at Amazon.

Research and make a list of the camera and other supplies you'll need to get started in analog photography. Many garage and yard sales have 1950s-1980s cameras for a song as well as online camera shops, which might be slightly more expensive but might have more pristine, guaranteed-to-work cameras. Also consider eBay—I've purchased three cameras, one of them an analog 1980s 35mm, that worked well and was a bargain because the user was moving and needed more space. There are some real deals on analog cameras out there, if you shop and compare. (The one exception is the Leica, arguably my dream camera and, as one photographer friend once said, "Nobody ever lowers the price or gets rid of them it seems.") You might also rent or borrow (the cheapest and perhaps best of all option) from friends, family, or a school near you; this is an especially great option for trying out several lo-fi cameras to find your best camera-type match before purchasing later.

Introverts: check online for a virtual class or group (such as at Flickr or Instagram) to join for camaraderie and to expand your skills. Flickr and Instagram are free, while (for a nominal, one-time fee) CreativeLive has several awesome analog classes (pre-recorded) that are loaded with tips and techniques to try, without class-mate interaction.

Extroverts: check out classes at local junior colleges, universities, or community centers. Join a camera club or start your own. Meet once a month for potlucks, snacks, or coffee and then take your cameras on an outing.

Save Everything: To Delete in Camera or Not to Delete, That is the Question

My friend N's son caught her throwing away some of his art the other day. Oopsie.

Feeling a little guilty as she stood by the "circular file" in the laundry room, she launched into an immediate save-face speech. "Of course I love all of your drawings, and we have your cool green folder to save many of your favorites, remember? You just tell me when you have a special one, and we can put it into the folder for later."

No judgment here (I have way too much stuff I don't use in storage to point fingers), but the kid wasn't having it.

"But that was a really good dinosaur," as he gazed up with puppy-dog eyes set to make any parent gulp.

Uh-oh. Tack two: "It really is, and I like that you chose such a happy red for him ... But you make a LOT of drawings every week, sooooo many." She held out her arms in a bid for joviality.

"Mama, it's a *girl!* She has a bow." Don't argue hairstyles with a four-year-old.

"Oh, yes, I see it now." Ahem. Tack three: "It's a wonderful dinosaur. I tell you what, let's save this one to mail to Pop-Pop."

Assuaged, the son nodded. I never asked if the drawing made its way to the folder, to the grandparent(s), or back into the garbage can.

Deciding to use this as a great chance to discuss pack-ratism and the value of sorting as well as giving things we no longer need away, N launched into the "We can't save everything, but we can save some things" lecture.

"Mama," he interrupted her, "I know, I know, you always say that." Then he scampered away while she decided, from now on, to chuck the accumulated torn coloring-book pages and squiggly doodles while he was still in class at pre-school.

This is probably one of many reasons I don't have children; I would hoard ... I mean *save* ... ALL of the drawings and drown in a paper and mouse dropping avalanche by the time they were teens. (My own mom still has most of the drawings I made in elementary school; I certainly wasn't then, nor am I now, a Rembrandt, so it must be the love.) I have a large see-through plastic box where I've kept the drawings and cards my young nieces have made for me in the past seven years. I mean every one. I don't know if it's because I've always been a paper-lover, the fact that I'm a writer and know the inherent value of written communication, because it's so unpopular to get snail-mail anymore that most of us who remember it thirst for it, or that I'm a giant softie when it comes to my darling nieces (yeah, all of this and more), but I can't part with even one piece.

Most of us artistic types are savers of some sort. We may save quite tangible items—first shoes, sentimental figurines, dog tags, jewelry given by friends and family to commemorate a certain occasion—or we might save intangible memories that have formed us and, although past, are nonetheless evocative. We save things that might be fun to look back on some day (although we rarely do) or that symbolize a time of pain, hurt, or questioning that we want to remind ourselves we've moved through successfully and learned from in some ways.

Nothing is ever wasted when it comes to making art. At the same time, we live during a highly digitalized, throw-away culture, where in-camera deleting is so easy as to be done almost automatically. I got you: sometimes, it just makes sense to let disappointing output go.

Before you press delete, though, give yourself a few moments to consider the following.

- **Is there an image in the shot that makes it symbolic, resonating to more than just one viewer?** For instance, a shot of a wedding dress hanging alone by a window (even if it's, say, your grandmother's or cousin's wedding dress) will suggest many thematic ideas to viewers, even if they never meet the woman who wore the dress. In other words, if something in the shot has cultural or communal ties, it will likely mean something to many viewers (although the meaning might be different for each viewer), and then odds are good that you should keep and play with this photographic concept longer.

- **Is the lighting generally good in the shot? What about the angle? Or, could both be improved?** If so, before you decide to delete, snap a few more shots, and compare them later, on-screen, where you can scrutinize with more details and a bigger screen.

- **Is something clearly missing from this shot that would make it better?** Maybe the above wedding dress, now years old, suggests unhappiness and loneliness but you wanted it to suggest the opposite. Furthermore, an idea occurs for your cousin to wear it again and then to create a before-and-long-after series with several former brides and to write a photo essay detailing what they were thinking on that day compared to what they are thinking wearing the gown again. In that case, you've got work to do and have launched what could be an exciting, insightful idea. **After taking any photo, quickly ask yourself: what do I want viewers to take away from this shot? What's the main emotion and idea it evokes?**

- **Sure, you might not use this shot again, but could it be useful to remind yourself later of what you've learned *doesn't* work? If it was a**

thoughtless error, such as your fingertip in the frame, no problem—delete away. It happens. But if the photo might help your learning curve, keep it. Memory cards (SD and SDHC) are relatively cheap (and getting cheaper each year) and store hundreds (if not thousands) on a whisper-tiny surface. **If in doubt, my motto is to save and sort later.**

Speaking of which, in my photography practice, I generally don't delete in-camera except for three reasons: the lighting is horrible (by far the number one reason I delete) or the shot is blurry or not the angle I wanted.

Even photos that I've almost deleted I was glad I saved later, when I created a photo collage with them or realized, "Hey, that wasn't half as bad as I thought. Just a few tweaks here and there and …" after some digital software magic, what I would have junked was salvageable after all.

Of course, not all images become art, and you won't print out many of them on a desk or give them a special space on your social-media wall. Still, it's good to keep in mind the above guidelines when perusing through the masses of shots from a shoot (I often take sixty or eighty at time, so I identify and screen-grab what appears to be the best and discard the rest fairly quickly), to ensure I don't spend all day hem-hawing at the computer.

Try this Prompt! Today, you'll take a series of photos of a sentimental object you or someone you know has saved. (If you like the wedding dress idea above, go for it!) Make sure the viewer can tell why the item is important or special aspects for why a person might save it. You might take a photo with the owner of the object (a self-portrait if that owner is you) or choose to photograph it alone. Then, run your photos through the above four guidelines before deciding if any should hit the cutting-room floor.

Restriction Station: Working around Common Yellow Lights and Red Flags

No homecoming queen for this one, and *sound the Debbie-Downer horn!*

Fair warning: this is probably not going to be the most popular article in this book for most readers (the author, too, raises her hand).

As artists, none of us likes to think about restrictions. It goes against the very nature of being makers who savor the sweet zing of discovery—I hear you and I agree. There's nothing worse than being felled by the dreaded internal editor before even picking up a camera.

This isn't about critical self-talk, though. It would do us well to reflect on a few considerations *before* setting our boundless creativity loose (and I'm all for that) on a world that is neither ideal, supportive, nor always up for being the subject of our lens curiosity.

Melanie: Will there be people in your photos?

Fellow Photographer: Yes, sometimes.

M: Do you personally know these subjects? Have they given permission for the photos to run as you see fit, for example on social media?

FP: Yeah, I know them. We talked about it. They're game. Why do I need to get written permission?

M: While you won't always need release forms when taking photos of people—street photography springs to mind—there are definitely times when it can be a wise idea, not only for you but for the people in your photos, to go into the shoot signing release forms, even if you don't think you'll need them. That way, later, you can avoid hurt feelings or lawsuits.

FP: Yeah, but when in the world would I need such forms? It's a royal pain to haul them around, and it's embarrassing to email and ask them to sign such a form when they've already been cool enough to agree to model?

M: I know the forms slow down the process. It's one of the reasons why I often shoot still-life, food, or nature imagery. Still, there are restrictions for still-life images, too, such as if you're taking shots of a trade-marked product or logos, which are also no-noes without company permission.

FP: Ugh. If you say so.

M: I hear you. Knowing what we're free to photograph without push back can get hella complicated. But there are ways to get around trademark problems. You can peel a label away or turn the product's label or logo away from the camera. Or blur it in software. Or use a generic stand-in.

But getting back to your photos with people in them; there's something amazing about great human-infused photography. Here's an example for when it could be wise to go ahead with the forms: maybe you've taken a breathtaking shot at an engagement or wedding or birth, but when you post it on your Instagram there are hurt feelings because the participants wanted to be the first, or only, ones to post photos of their happiest moments. Or (and it sometimes happens) they don't like the photo you chose to share with the world because of something that seems picky to you but huge to them. Best case scenario, they email you to take down the shot—that's also embarrassing and hurtful for the artist who sees only beauty and joy in their shot and really wants to share their skills (spoiler alert: I've had the "really don't want you sharing that photo" email happen to me—ick and double ick). Much better, in my mind, *not* to have to backpedal with egg on your face, so to speak.

Sometimes, for whatever reason and it's certainly not fair, people change their minds. If you have it in writing, it's fair game and yours to decide what to do with, whichever way you decide to run with the photos. If you don't have it in writing, it's their word against yours and it might turn ugly. Again, this is worst-case scenario stuff, but worst cases do happen to somebody—far better not to have it be you and your art.

FP: Okay, yeah, I can see your point. I don't like it, but I can see it …

M: Where will your photos be taken?

FP: Why should that matter?

M: Well, it matters more than you'd think sometimes.

Say you meet a friend at a local café or restaurant that has a gorgeous brick-wall backdrop and Parisian-style wrought-iron furniture with those little curlicues to die for …

FP: I love that stuff!

M: Me, too. It looks amazing on film (although not the most comfortable).

FP: Totally.

M: So you're going to take photos at this café, right? Well, many businesses poo-poo that idea. They don't want photographers taking up space, causing a scene, and conducting business while they are in the middle of *their* business on a property [that] they pay high rents on. See where this is headed?

FP: Yeah. I guess I didn't think of it that way. I mean, I've purchased the raspberry scone and two cappuccinos; I'm a paying customer like everyone else. I guess I thought I had a right to be there.

M: You do have a right to be there … to drink your drink and nibble the pastry, but that doesn't include the right to take photos in the minds of café customers and employees. Better, instead, to call or (even better) make an in-person visit to the owner and/or employees a few days or over a week *before* you want to take your photos. Explain in detail who you are (a business card and/or website pulled up so you can show them your work on your phone would come in really handy for this), why you love their location and support their business regularly, as well as the kind of project shoot you'll do and how little time and space you estimate it would take.

Some business owners work out deals with photographers. For instance, they ask that the photographer visit on an off-day (such as a late Tuesday afternoon, rather than a Saturday morning) for a certain amount of time only (say, twenty minutes in, out, and thank you). Other business owners will agree to such personal project shoots if you offer to give them several shots for promotion of their business for free. Could be a good trade.

Sometimes, though, it will be a no-go. It's a bummer, but acceptance, a thanks, and your back-up plan destination is your go-to then. For every shoot idea, it's a good rule of thumb (unless you or your family own the property) to pick three or four possible locations where the same shots could bloom, just in case.

FP: Couldn't I just sneak in with my iPhone? It doesn't even look like a camera, and people take selfies all of the time. How are they going to stop me?

M: True—smartphone cameras are awesomely discreet and also take amazing shots. That brings up a great topic. Ethics of art! Tricky—I told you this wasn't going to be a walk in the park. Far be it from me to tell you or any other artist what you can or cannot do. In the end, you have your own morals and ethics to follow. I'm listing tips and guidelines but follow your own heart and conscience.

That said, it's likely you or your client will end up posting the photos somewhere online, likely tagging you and your business/social-media pages. The owners might not find out during the shoot, but they won't appreciate learning about it afterwards. Best case: you find another coffee joint. Worst case: you get a reputation for being sneaky or worse. Clients and businesses who might have otherwise worked with you will pause or decide not to do so. My thought, however tempting it is (and I, too, have found it tempting): if you wouldn't want it done to you, don't do it to someone else.

FP: Well, that's annoying.

M: Yeah, I know. I'm sorry. Like I said: I hate to bear any news that might restrict the flow of great photography entering the world, but I do want you to be prepared. Just in case.

FP: So if my subjects are going to be finicky and I can't get the location I want, why bother?

M: Good news: even though it initially stinks, there will be plenty of subjects who either won't need the release or who will happily sign it and trust your artistic talents. Ditto with locations. For those who aren't, there are plenty of other locales and subjects to shoot. Take a perusal through some of these other chapters to get more ideas. The sky's the limit.

Stay open to taking your initial idea and tweaking a few of the details. Figuring out ways around restrictions while holding onto the general flavor of your initial idea is an opportunity for your creativity to amp up a notch or two. You might end up with work that surprises you in the best of ways.

FP: Or a complete dud.

M: Or a complete *stunner*.

FP: (Eye roll.) Didn't somebody wake up on the sunny side of the bed?

M: (Enigmatic smile.) Keep going. And going. Think how long it took to invent the light bulb, the fridge, the polio vaccine, but somebody kept trying. You will, too.

FP: Peace out.

Try this Prompt!
Make a list of a few fun locations—parks, restaurants, cafes, stores—within an hour of your home. Pick one of the locations and write about your dream shoot at that location for fifteen minutes. Who would be your subject? List four or five areas of the location you would use for your shots. This might be a great time to take a location-scouting jaunt to notice special out-of-the way spots that could really inspire your Muse. Take your notes (and your business card and website portfolio link) to the location and strike up a friendly conversation with the staff to float the idea of your taking photos there, complete with your specific ideas and an estimate of how long it might take. Offer free promotional shots in exchange, if you feel they are amenable and it's something you'd like to do. You might be surprised by a yes. If a no is forthcoming, no worries! Proceed to prompt #2.

Try this Prompt, the reboot! Congratulations! You've been told no and both you AND your idea are still breathing. A little challenge or twenty falls into the life of every artist. Sit back down with your journal and write about alternate locations where your dream shoot can still take place for fifteen or twenty minutes because it's going to. What backgrounds and backdrops from your first location (such as trees, a fence, and a lake) might also be present at a second, third, and even fourth location. If you can't think of any, call in your lifelines: post online (people love giving tips) or text family and friends for their location ideas. You'll likely learn of a few new places to explore and snag a just-as-good locale this way. Within two weeks of your no, get out to your alternate location and make it happen (snagging permission first, of course). Challenge accepted? Good. Go!

Writing about Our Art

"THE CAMERA IS AN INSTRUMENT THAT TEACHES PEOPLE HOW TO SEE WITHOUT A CAMERA." – DOROTHEA LANGE

- **Choose dynamic nouns, adjectives, and verbs:** Instead of "special" or "interesting," terms that may have different meanings depending on the audience, try: "vibrant" or "pin-striped." Diction choices that denote color or shade, shape, size, texture, or mood/tone are particularly good options.

- **Be specific:** Robert Henri wrote, "We are instinctively blind to what is not relative. We are not cameras. We select." Why should the audience care about this piece? What makes it distinctive? **Why did you choose to take a photo of this particular detail or object? What did you omit or find unnecessary to the image? What makes your image modern or what makes it reminiscent of another time or place?**

- **Compare this image to other images readers may be familiar with.** How is it like another famous artist's or writer's work? What qualities does it share? How does this image take the other idea and push it further or in a new direction?

- **Contrast this image or idea to other images.** How is it different from what we've seen artists and writers create before? List some examples.

- **Was there anything you cropped or left out of the image?** If so, what was it and why did you do so?

- **Backstory, backstory, backstory. Explore why you made the choices you did while composing the image.** Let's face it: in our busy-busy-busy lives, we often rely on gut instincts and quick choices to snap a picture or begin a new piece of writing. There's nothing wrong with that. In fact, work with it! Now that you've taken the image, go back and ask yourself why this subject interested you. Break it down into details about where you were when you came across this subject or decided to pose this person or object for your lens, what specific part or parts of this subject resonate with you, who this image is meant to interest, and any other details you think the audience would find intriguing. For example, maybe you were on your way to the parking lot after a long day of teaching when you noticed that caterpillar crawling across the cracked sidewalk outside your academic building. You dodged thirty-five fifteen-year-olds to pull out your camera phone to capture its undulating wiggle over the crack while said fifteen-year-olds watched and whipped out their camera phones, too. Incidentally, true story.

- **Make connections. Note if this image is a one-off or part of a series. Also describe what initially appealed to you about this subject.** While it's not as obvious as other details, it can be just as evocative to mention whether you've been exploring this red sand pail over the course of a year or if you just took one shot of it when your grandson was playing one afternoon. In a series, images are meant to work in concert or apart, while seemingly one-off or random snaps carry their own meaning and might have connections to your other artistic pursuits. Maybe you've been writing and photographing about the sea for many years and this sand bucket actually has more in common with your other art than you'd first thought.

Top Ten Guidelines for Creating a Sensational Photo Series

Much like short stories in an anthology or individual poems in a collection, photography has the power to develop narrative pizzazz, one piece at time and then later collated together. Many literary magazines, in fact, seek work that is linked.

Apply these straightforward guidelines as you launch and explore your own series.

- **Choose a subject or theme before you pick up your camera.** Knowing ahead of time what you are seeking will train your photographic eye to narrow and spot the kinds of images that will fit together as a unit. It will also help you to save time, as the images you shoot will more likely fit together than if you randomly snapped a wide variety; while staying open to possibilities is still important, for developing a series focusing and zeroing in are even more important.

- **Choose your angle. What is the purpose of your series?** To draw attention to a social issue? To explain how something like food or a craft is made, step-by-step? To demonstrate the diversity and range of the topic? To bring out a never-before-documented quality about your subject? To juxtapose your subject with something or someone else? **Jot a few notes about your main goals and hopes for taking these photos.**

- **Choose your ideal location.** Would outdoor or indoor locales enhance your subject best? Be as specific as you can; instead of at *a park*, plan for *Jones Park at 2:00 p.m. because the lighting then is bright and direct.*

- **Schedule it in. Set a shoot date, as professional photographers do.** Plan ahead a few hours or days for most places, unless you own the land/workshop/studio where you'll shoot; otherwise, prepare to rent or ask permission for your locale, from weeks, months, or even a year in advance if your series will be a birth, engagement, or wedding series. Prepare, as much as you can, for an alternative plan if outdoors, in case of inclement weather. For some shoots, rain, snow, wind, and other conditions will add to the series, such as for fun family portraits while making snow forts; for others, you'll need to reschedule for a better-weather day. Even if your series will be a still-life series in your own personal room or studio, think about your setup. Do you have a tripod at the ready? Do you have a place to collect and gather your materials and to store them afterwards? Is your table/workspace near a natural source of light or do you have or need to buy/borrow artificial lighting? Be as practical and direct as possible, and anticipate possible obstructions with a Plan B, C, or even D. In the park example above, random parades or government holidays could create a busier scene than expected or a shut-down. Not all shoots will require a lot of time ahead to plan, especially if they can take place in your own apartment, home, or studio—I've had many shoots that were carried out within the afternoon or even just an hour—but it's best for most series shoots off-site to give yourself significant time to organize and anticipate.

- **Make a (visual) plan, Stan. Some artists sketch four or five main idea frames, like a story board, detailing props or subjects and light-source direction details and more. Other creators jot a little list of possible types of shots using words.** Whether you sketch or jot, preparing a practical game plan for how the many pieces of the shoot will fit together is a sound idea.

- **But don't become so bogged down by the plan that you miss great shots on the fly. Enter with some specific ideas—yes. Stick to the plan 100%—no.** Be open to on-the-spot opportunities and serendipity. If something better comes up, roll with it.

- **Consider before and after, otherwise known as cause and effect. Planning the practical "befores," such as the equipment, the idea list or drawings, and model releases and permissions for location(s) if needed, helps to ensure an easier "after" of post-processing that is hassle-free for you. Another way you can consider before and after is that many series show a change in the subject over time.** Keep in mind that not all series are a one-shoot-and-done premise. I've seen series that covered, a year, five, ten, even more than twenty years of children or fur babies growing up, parents becoming grandparents, journeys of addiction or renewal/healing, and numerous moves across country or continents. What will serve your subject best? A short-documentation timeframe (of just one shoot, or over a few weeks or months) will suit some subjects (such as the preparation of a favorite meal or a graduation day) while other subjects will be better served by ongoing shoots over much longer. If your series will require more than a year to complete, at what intervals will you recommence shooting? Will you take a shot on a particular anniversary/birthday, quarterly, by season, or play it by ear at random intervals when the mood strikes?

- *Beginning, middle, end* **is never a bad way to go. It works in fiction and nonfiction. It can't hurt in a photo series, either.** Plan how, in eight or ten photos, you would denote a starting point/

catalyst, rising-action points, the mid-way climax, and a falling-action/denouement/afterward. Make sure to shoot more photos than your goal of eight or ten (or fewer) that you'll end up submitting. I often shoot sixty or seventy at least to later pick my top six or eight that mesh well.

- **Omit any photos that repeat an already-expressed idea. Subtle variations aren't enough in a series. Each shot must propel the theme forward in a linked but unique way.** For instance, if you plan to take a series with the purpose of highlighting the importance of the local youth soccer league to inspire business donations to support the team, two shots of the same player would be redundant as would two shots of the same position on the field. A better approach would include a variety of shots—perhaps one with the team and their coach during a pep talk before the game, one mid-field shot during the intense action of the match, and one near the goal or even some player close-ups of smiles, high-fives, fancy footwork or team jerseys. Or perhaps a close-up shot of the faded, old jerseys to encourage donations for replacement uniforms.

- **Play up unifying elements. Tints, black and white, filters, and similar cropping or camera angles can underscore that these separate shots work well as a single unit.** For a series, if I submit one monochromatic shot, I make sure they're all black-and-white shots in my submission.

Some literary magazines ask for color shots or don't state a preference, while others request *only* black and white, macro instead of micro shots, and other specifications. **Always check editorial guidelines before submitting.**

Try this
Prompt! Make a list of three or four possible series topics. Pick your favorite one and follow the ideas through the above steps, including a free-write of your main ideas, and then go for it. When you're finished taking the series, research some markets actively seeking photo series and submit your work. Much of the purpose and joy of creating a series is sharing your work with an audience.

Even if your series will take weeks, months, or even years to complete, editors and viewers are still interested in unfinished, in-progress series as well—just note that the series is "ongoing" and submit away!

Section Three: Getting Your Art Out There

To the Benevolent Stranger Who Bought My First Art Print

When it was time to decide if I would pay the relisting fees, I almost didn't. The photos (twenty of them, a variety of still-life, nature, and aquatic prints) had been sitting on the craft site for nearly five months with nary a buyer, despite my mentioning them on guest blogs and in artist interviews that ran in literary magazines publishing a few of the prints and other images.

Why bother relisting? Perhaps it was just another fun, wild-hair amusement and not meant to be. I'd taken my Christmas money and bought an entry-level professional printer, so I still got to practice my printing skills with photos my sister emailed of my darling nieces, whether or not anyone bought a thing.

Well, why not? Just one more time.

I clicked to renew them all, and then went back to regularly scheduled programming. For five weeks.

Then the email arrived. *Congratulations on your sale.*

Your order number is 59279488204. My own photo-graph stared back at me. I'd sold a print!

No, a confetti party didn't descend from my ceiling game-show style and I didn't spring around my room pumping my fists in glory—but I wanted to, oh how I wanted to.

Yes, my profit was a handsome $15. Well, less after figuring in the listing fees, supplies (including fancy German archival paper that's as smooth as butter), inks, and a new printer, but in terms of motivation and encouragement, in terms of underscoring that someone unrelated to me and unfamiliar with me had scrolled a crafting site with approximately a gajillion users, endless kwatillions (I'm not a math major) of them offering myriad photos, and you chose to press the button to order a 5 x 7 of my jellyfish print—that's a priceless divi-dend. (Check out the PDF photo file at melaniedfaith. com/photography-for-writers for photo #16.)

Your purchase out-of-the-blue uplifted me in a way only winning the lottery or holding my nieces for the first time could possibly compare. Speaking of my nieces, it took everything I had in me not to mention in the card I wrote with your print that I took this photo at my nieces' first trip to an aquarium when they visited last summer.

Your purchase, my friend, kept me smiling while I carefully printed, signed, and addressed your print and then tucked in a rather formal thank you that in no way expresses the effusive, frothy rush from your nod to me as an artist with your pocket change and your choice. You chose mine, and that's not a feeling too-soon forgotten.

So, no, I won't be putting a down-payment on a house

with my earnings or visiting my print in a gilt frame in a museum, but to me, the print has gone to somewhere just as remarkable: to a wall in an apartment in a great, impersonal city where someone has decided that out of all of the art you could possibly wish to feature in your personal space, mine is the one that you most want to see.

The writer in me smiles to think of the title I gave the image long before I listed the print for sale: "Rise." Rise, indeed.

Try this Prompt! Write a letter to someone who has, wittingly or unwittingly, encouraged your development as an artist.

Bonus Prompt! Brainstorm ways you can encourage an artist in your own life. Buy a self-published memoir? Schedule the first photography session from a new shutterbug? It is no small thing to break out your pocket change to support another artist-in-progress with some monetary encouragement. You might be the difference between someone throwing in the towel or continuing to create.

On Saving a Nurturing Space for Yourself

"ART IS NOT THE POSSESSION OF THE FEW WHO ARE RECOGNIZED WRITERS, PAINTERS, MUSICIANS; IT IS THE AUTHENTIC EXPRESSION OF ANY AND ALL INDIVIDUALITY. THOSE WHO HAVE THE GIFT OF CREATIVE EXPRESSION IN UNUSUALLY LARGE MEASURE DISCLOSE THE MEANING OF THE INDIVIDUALITY OF OTHERS TO THOSE OTHERS." — JOHN DEWEY

Save this chapter for the doomy days when a little screed rolls through your head, a gloomy gray rain cloud, that goes a little something like this: *Why even bother? What's left to say? Millions of people post their photos online. Millions more call themselves photographers and have websites. What can I possibly create that isn't already out there, and who would care anyway? People only glance, click, and scroll.*

- **Take heart. We've all been there.** If you've been practicing artistic mediums for numerous years, as I have with my writing and photography, you've surely gone through cycles both of high-spirited artistic inspiration and creation and the flip-side: long, dark days of blah and doubt if you'll ever pick up your pen or camera again. After selling my first art print, I didn't sell another again for six months. Selling and/or publishing creative work is highly competitive and certainly not a straight-uphill trajectory, even once you've sold or published a few times.

- **You have plenty of company.** Think of it: we are not computers or robots that work mechanically. There's a great deal of mystery, motivation, and serendipity involved in both photography and writing. They are crafts in which artists spend lifetimes learning, developing, and growing. **You will never be perfect or 100% in control, and that's a good thing.**

- I have participated in daily challenges for both photography and writing. During those periods, I produce a consistent and large amount of new shots or pieces, not all of them publishable but many of them leading me in slightly new or unexpected directions that shine a light on themes and ideas I hadn't realized I'd been grappling with until then.

- I'll also be honest—**I have also gone through periods where I haven't picked up my camera in weeks**, where it just sat on my desk or in a drawer, waiting for that tug of creativity. During the fallow periods, it's way easier for me to go down the "why-bother?" route than when I am writing or photographing a few times a week or when I'm swapping with a friend regularly or completing a challenge.

- **Don't let the fallow times fool you: they are as necessary as the times of large productivity.** As artists, we get discouraged when we compare our output or our projects that are stalled to what we see or read online. **Small spurts without photographing or writing are healthy and normal; what's not the best for us is comparing others' highlight reels and posts to our standstill. That tends to lead to prolonged periods of inactivity, which certainly *isn't* good for our creative process.**

- **Give yourself planned social-media rests or, at the least, limit how much time you spend perusing others' photographs and playing the art-comparison game.** Hey, I fully understand: just yesterday, I logged into two of my social-media accounts (one where I post photographs) and two hours later, I looked up, aghast, that I'd just dumped one hundred and twenty minutes into scrolling, liking, and commenting. It's all-too-easy to fall down the rabbit hole, so to speak, and Alice, you're gonna have to dig yourself out of there before the Queen of Hearts mutters her famous line about losing heads. Other days, like today, I literally set a kitchen timer. Whatever I can peruse, post, and comment on in twenty minutes, great—when that timer dings: sayonara, social media.

- Speaking of social media, one of my favorite on-line photographers posted this little gem along with a home-interiors shot that deeply resonated: "I love social media, but sometimes it's good to just live life and not document every second of it." Yes, yes, and yes. **It's wonderful to have an audience, yo, but we need to borrow a little pre-internet-age common sense. Share as a simple and pleasing process, and then swiftly go … back to a personal, private life.**

- **Save a little for yourself; save a little for your art. Photography and writing both need room to breathe. I've found, as an innate giver, Type A list-maker workaholic, and introvert, that I must hold back a portion of my photos, writing, and life details for myself.** As much as I love audience-building and connection, having that little ego boost when my photos and writings are appreciated by others, I also savor carving out my own behind-the-scenes that very few are invited to see. It's vital that I practice self-care so that I can take the pressure off of myself and just live.

- **Nothing else has been quite so nourishing to my artistic process as figuring out what and how much to share.** While I frequently email, respond, and send literary resources daily, at least six days a week, for my students during the school year, I update my personal website melaniedfaith. com/blog and Instagram instagram.com/write-path99 just three times a month on average. That doesn't sound like much, but it adds up in a blog and/or feed over time to create a nice portfolio and glimpse into my writing and photography practice and publications, without taking over my personal life or releasing projects before they are ready for their audience. Also, last summer I took a break from Facebook (letting everyone know in a post) and logged in just one or two times in all of mid-July through August while spending time with my darling nieces offline. That renewal was splendid and refreshing, and I got a ton of personal writing done, including some chapters in this book.

- But guess what? I'm still, like all of you, figuring it out as I go. I can tell you that I have shared more glimpses of my personality and daily life in this book and in my two previous craft books for writers than I have in all of my creative work combined, which is great for my artistic growth, but has sometimes also worn me thinner than I prefer. I've still overshared sometimes, on social media and in emails, too. Have I realized I sometimes left little energy for myself? **Sure; it happens. I proceed forward afterward, adjusting and knowing more of what to keep a nurturing, private space for myself and my art next time.**

- Speaking of my craft books: do you think I didn't think about the fact that there is a market flooded with craft books about writing for writers before, during, and after writing mine? I sure did, numerous times. Did I dwell on that or let it stop me? Nope. **Just because it has been done before, even hundreds or thousands of times, that shouldn't be a dead-end for you. Challenge yourself to bring something utterly authentic and completely *you* to the composition or page.**

- **Each person is different in how much they feel like sharing and knowing where their own boundaries reside** (I'm an introvert, so I recharge my batteries with time alone to write or read or photograph or watch movies), **but I've yet to meet an artist who *didn't* benefit from at least some unplanned, unposted time to live and reflect independently.** Some of my private thoughts and conversations between just one friend have led to very enriching art that, if I'd jumped to share with everyone in my network, likely never would have happened otherwise.

Some reminders that I've found useful on down days in my own creative process with photography and writing:

- **This is practice, not a performance. Take the pressure off of yourself.** Feel free to share a small quantity of your work in a meaningful way, online and offline, but save something for the pleasure of making in itself.

- **Small breaks are just as important as high-volume challenges to developing as an artist. Give**

the well a little time to refill now and again; as long as it's not a permanent standstill, you'll be just fine and your art will likely grow for the breathing room.

- Creating is fun. Even if you never share any of the work you make (which is highly unlikely), **there should be an element of play and self-study in your pieces.** Follow flits of ideas as they occur to you.

- **Don't stop to judge yourself;** go with your hunch and any little spark that crosses your mind. See where it leads. **If it leads to nothing or nothing you like, no harm done.**

- **Schedule an art date with yourself.** Write it in your schedule as you would any appointment, show up without expectations or distractions (turn off your phone—I promise, you won't perish without checking for a few hours), get a sitter, write. Be astonished that it is that simple and that hard simultaneously.

- Realize that much like exercise, getting enough sleep, and good nutrition, practicing an **art can sometimes be a slog and a drag. (What isn't?) Then again, the mental, emotional, and even physical benefits from creating are enough encouragement to keep progressing.**

Try this Prompt! Journal today from the POV of your doubting voice for ten minutes. Then, flip the script. Journal for ten more minutes in which a calmer, more positive voice refutes each Debbie Downer drawback and put forward reasons why you have the skills to embrace the normal ups and downs of a creative practice.

At the end of the exercise, print out and rip up the negative, doubting voice's passage. Print and save the positive journaling post. You've got this, through all obstructions, breaks, and doubts.

Tips for
Selective Sharing

What do you think of when you read the word "vulnerable?" Something or someone shaky? Tenderness? Someone unsure or ambivalent? Nakedness?

Among the fifteen definitions for "naked" at dictionary. com, the eleventh one resonates best with the artistic journey: "exposed to view or plainly revealed." Let's be real: it is often terrifying to express ourselves as creators to a wide audience. I have had borderline nausea and near panic attacks before the release of several of my creative projects, especially books. Once you know that your brain children are headed into the turbulent waters of the internet and permanently emblazoned on shelves in print, without your loving guidance to explain or stand up for them, it's enough to make a person never share another creative venture with anyone again.

The world at large likes to see creatives as one-trick ponies who fit into whatever impression they have of us at any given time or in a certain social or work group, and when that idea has been altered after experiencing our art, the resulting cold shoulder or downright hurtful reactions can be devastating to artists. Ironically, it often takes a sensitive, empathetic visionary intelligence to create images that resonate with an audience while, at the same time, the sharing of this art demands a hide as thick as a rhinoceros, to paraphrase prose-writer Flannery O'Connor, and the ability to shoulder an Atlas-worthy burden of bad press, caustic comments, and confused or plain-old apathetic reactions to what felt magical and precious in our imaginations, our lens, our Muse in the midst of the making process.

How to reconcile the need to make something personally expressive and evocative with the wrenching strictures of society is a conundrum for the ages. While each artist must decide how much they feel comfortable sharing and, truthfully, the pendulum for how little or how much to share depends upon many factors (the least of which include: the communities in which you live, the nature/strictness of your day job, and your own personality), **here are some tips I've found useful when navigating the how-much-to-share conundrum of being a productive, publishing writer and photographer:**

- **The Selective Sharing Exercise:** Instead of releasing a whole series of photos or a large album of photo files at once, choose one or two and wait for feedback before sharing more.

- **The Selective Withholding Exercise:** Sometimes, we feel as if we need to share every piece of work we've created, or we share our latest work only to get negative or no feedback in return. It's perfectly fine, and in some cases preferable, to hold back work or to make work solely for your own joy. If you're unsure about your work or just beginning to explore new ideas in a photo series, feel free to sleep on it and give it more thought and time before sharing. It is always your work, and you should do with it whatever makes you feel most comfortable. There's always the possibility that you'll want to share the work later—pace yourself and stay open to this idea if it appeals. On the other hand, it might be possible that you'll decide this series doesn't need the light of day and just leads you to other, newer work that you will want to share without hesitation—that's fine, too.

- **The Work-Your-Way-Up Approach:** I totally understand why releasing your work on Instagram or in an online magazine, where it might hover for months or years and be open to a mixed bag of comments, could scare an artist into never sharing with anyone again. I've had a few nasty trolls comment on and misunderstand my work and, while it didn't make me stop publishing, it stung. Sharing your work offline, with a trusted friend or fellow artist who is at roughly the same stage of artistic development as you can be a fantastic way to dip your toe into the pond of sharing your work in a safe and meaningful manner. Choose your favorite piece and, if you feel up to it, share a few details of what inspired you to take this photo. **Friends and fellow artists generally show enthusiasm and support for what you've created and why it has resonance for you.** Their questions and praise frequently lead to encouragement for sharing with a slightly larger audience in the future or deepens the feeling that, while one's art might not resonate with everyone, it does have significance and should continue to be created. Or a friend's reaction of confusion might be a reminder to continue to work on our art before sharing again.

- **The Artistic-Tribe Approach:** Sometimes, your friends, family, or coworkers won't be your best audience or won't get why you are creating what you are. One of the reasons I went to grad school for my MFA is that I wanted to study my writing craft with a school-full of people who had the same artistic goals as I did. There is power in numbers. You don't necessarily have to apply to an art school or summer program to find your tribe, although those two venues might work well. Many schools and camps have short-term (one-week, one-month, one-year) residencies or conferences (some as short as a weekend or even just a day or afternoon). Live in a rural community or don't have the money to travel to meet fellow creatives? No problem. Many groups and classes online, both noncredit and credit, are free or nearly so, and for an investment of time, energy, and candor, you might meet a pal or two to share your work and discuss the joys and challenges of your craft on a monthly, weekly, or as-needed basis. You might also start a photography group that meets once a month at a local café, bookstore, or your home and make the photographic equivalent of beta readers through such groups. The fact that digital photography is so widespread and practically everyone is online and has a camera on their phone these days will make it easy to stay in touch and share images and meeting times/reminders. Social media also offers unique opportunities if you think outside the box. Have a favorite Insta photographer whose work you admire? **Send a friendly, short email; many buddies informally begin with short emails or texts and, over time and with patience, become great fans and encouragers of each other. Photographers and writers are two of the most friendly, generous groups of people with their scant spare time that I've ever met.** If you never hear back, however, try not to take it personally: there are only so many hours in a day. Move on to your next favorite photographer and reach out with a compliment and note that you, too, are a photographer. You never know.

In the end, whether you publish frequently, share once a month with one trusted friend, workshop with a group, or labor on your own for years before you want to share your photographs, it is always up to you. You are a photographer; you are a brave creator. No one can take that away from you.

Try this Prompt!
Taboo! Verboten! No-Nos! Write about a few of your photographic fears. Spend fifteen or twenty minutes jotting notes about reactions you dread to your work. Then make a list of three photographic subjects that feel out-of-bounds or dangerous to photograph. Nothing illegal or immoral, of course, but perhaps subjects that would surprise your mother-in-law or your coworkers or friends if they knew you were interested in taking photographs about this subject. Now: pick one. That's what you'll photograph today. Go!

Napoleon's Toothbrush & Other ARTifacts: On Selling Your Work

Napoleon Bonaparte's toothbrush has a handle made of silver that has burnished since 1795 to an almost golden hue. It has gorgeous gilt engravings carved just below the head of the skinny bristles made of—gulp!—horse hair, which is a dark mocha-almost brown. There is a capital N (of course, a large capital!) at the base of the brush, where the Emperor's little hand would clutch the brush. Above the N, which to my eyes resembles the N in Times New Roman font with extra, elegant thick cross-hatching in the middle of the letter, there rests an unmistakable illustration of a mini crown.

Napoleon didn't invent the toothbrush, of course: that honor goes (depending on whom you ask) to either the Chinese (who also invented toothpastes) or the Egyptians (if you consider frayed branch ends close enough to our modern-handled cleaning apparatus), but the fact that, way back then, Napoleon used such an everyday object that is so much a part of our lives interests many collectors.

In fact, numerous belongings of the famed egotistical emperor are hot commodities in recent auctions. In June 2018, a hat Napoleon supposedly wore at Waterloo went for $400,000 and earlier, in November 2014, another of Napoleon's tri-cornish dark-gray chapeaux brought $2.4 million to a South-Korean collector at a memorabilia auction. Pretty sweet dough for head coverings, non?

How much would this fetching toothbrush fetch? One estimate I found from over twenty years ago placed the price at $21,000 back then. The price is almost beside the point—it's no secret that objects that belong to the famous (political and spiritual leaders, Insta-famous stars, singers, and performers) often carry a hefty price tag. But what about what *we* have, namely: what we extraordinary-ordinary creators make?

What is a print photograph of ours worth? What about a digital file used for a website or a book cover? What would an editor or friend-of-a-friend-of-a-friend who we don't know in person be willing to pay for our artistic work, anyway, and how can we find those interested parties?

It can be enough to make a heady swimmy. I totally identify. This is one reason why I didn't venture into selling prints until about nine years *after* my first photos were published in literary magazines for free or, now and again, contributors' copies.

Once money is involved in any enterprise, unforeseen headaches abound.

Like you, I have several life events and responsibilities hopping at once. While I was still learning more about my photographic art and hustling my writing, I was also teaching for three schools part-time, trying to write a novel and numerous poems that became a poetry book, and launching a freelance-editing business. To divide myself into one more piece to figure out how much to charge for my photos—well, I liked my sanity a little too much for that!

What did I do? I kept taking photos for the fun of it, because it relaxed me and brought me joy, without expectations.

In due time, many months later, and through showing my art to friends and publishing for free in small literary presses, I made some networking connections who sent opportunities and tips my way that led to a few small-paying gigs, such as cover art for a few wonderful books. Although I'm a go-getter and motivator by nature, I've begun to pace myself and to narrow down what I can feasibly accomplish per day, per week, and per month, to avoid burnout and to see the long view of the exciting next options for my work as I've entered my thirties and forties. **That often translates to keep refining your narrow-down to make room for marvelous opportunities you never envisioned.**

Due to the widespread, excellent camera technology in our time, **the market is jam-packed with folks trying to make their passions make a buck**, so prepare for plenty of competition. Still, **we can take heart: we each have something utterly unique to show the world AND the times have never been**

more encouraging for creatives to float our art out there and actively pursue collectors or buyers.

Key word: active. If you're independent-minded, enthusiastic, and creative, you can make one or more options work to create a cash flow. At the same time, don't rush to quit your day job immediately; you'll likely need it for a while. Still, I want to encourage you not to ditch your daydream just because it will likely take extra effort and time to reach your goals.

Scope out the business sense of other photographers and learn what the going market rates are.

Before deciding the best next steps for you to pursue, have a chat with a photographer who sells their work. Even better: put your writing skills to work and interview photographers for your blog or website. Ask:

- How did they start to share their work?

- Who or what encouraged them to share their work?

- What steps did they take to make money from their shots?

- How much money they made the first few weeks and months.

- How do they balance professional (paying) work with (non-paying) passion projects?

- What steps did they take to get past rejection or lack of sales?

Take time to think, explore, research, and then launch. Still creative, still jazzy and enthusiastic, but *informed*.

If you don't know any artists personally, no worries—you can peruse and find plenty of get-started details online. I recommend seeing what visual artists on platforms like Etsy charge for a 5x7 or an 8x10 or larger. That's what I did.

- Peruse the sites of ten or fifteen artists and see if there are any common denominators for the price of prints.

- Pick the artwork most similar in quality to your own, and also factor in what you would feel comfortable selling each print for.

- Figure in the cost of your materials. If digital files, that cost is quite low: only an SD card and your camera costs or if you rent a location or other materials like a tripod, and, of course, your time; if print files, you also need to figure in the cost of your ink cartridges, archival-quality paper which can be quite pricey per sheet compared to writing printing paper, or the costs for an external lab to print and ship them.

- Is your main goal to make a profit *or* to send work into the world for others to appreciate? Is there a series of steps to accomplish both?

Great news: if you're organized and communicative, there are plenty of interested buyers for sporadic sales and you can reach them in numerous venues, from in-person to online.

A few popular options for advertising our visual creations for purchase:

- **Blogs and personal websites:** (my site includes a tab for my photography portfolio with examples of both published and unpublished work, as well as a link to my (drumroll, please) books and classes.

- **Instagram:** (I joined in August 2018 and have found it an excellent place to network and offer samples of my work—providing a more-frequently-updated photography portfolio which I link to my website photography portfolio via link).

- **Community art shows:** (colleges, universities, art schools, great exposure and networking with fellow artists).

- **Photostock companies online:** (to be competitive, prepare to list hundreds or more images at once, sorting by theme and listing by creative keywords so searchers will easily find your images).

- **Photo stock image-sharing sites** such as Unsplash (despite no payment, great exposure and a direct way to share your creativity for others' benefit).

- **Etsy:** (my preferred method for selling my art prints, although they take a listing fee and a cut.

I've made twenty-three sales so far and only expanded my shop to photographic prints a few months ago, so I'm still learning as I go. Still, slow but steady growth, and each print I send off to a buyer gives off a little zing of excitement for me and, I hope, for the buyer).

- **Literary magazines:** (so many independent and university-related magazines seek imagery to accompany their written art—these are unsung markets to get published, but it must be said that they often just pay in contributor's copies, a very small token payment of a few dollars, or sometimes just the thrill of seeing your byline and work online or in a print issue—heady stuff, for sure, but if you expect some kind of physical payment, this and the art shows often ain't it).

- **Facebook:** (cut out the middleman, often best for selling work to those you are already endeared to).

- **Twitter:** I've known about this site for ten years, but it took the encouragement of one of my publishers to help me to make the leap into Tweeting in December 2018. Catch my latest Tweets at twitter.com/writer_faith.

- **Consignment for local boutiques, restaurants, or shops who like to decorate their stores with local talents' wares.** You don't have to be there hardly at all, but potential customers will see your work over a period of weeks or months. One of my wonderful mentees and also a cousin have both done this to flourishing success in the two different rural communities where each lives.

These are by no means the only ways to spread the word about your work, whether monetized or not.

Apply some thinking-outside-the-box creativity: donate a photo print to the auction at your child's or grandchild's school fundraiser, for instance, or join (or start!) a monthly photo club to network and pool resources to other markets you might not have thought of, such as craft shows, festivals, even yard sales which abound in interested browsers who enjoy the chance to chat with the artist in person.

Try this
Prompt! Schedule that interview with a local photographer. Use the six questions I offer as a jumping-off point, and make sure to jot any other details you'd like to know and take notes on their responses. Keep in mind that each person's path is slightly different, so borrow the advice that make sense for your goals, who you'd like to share your art with, and set out on your own trail for the rest.

Don't know any local artists? Peruse Instagram, Flickr, and other photo websites—including the portfolios for magazines such as *B & W, Click,* and *SHOTS* (which often includes the websites and/or emails for their artists). Contact one of the online or print-magazine photographers you admire, and inquire if you can interview them, either via email or phone/Skype within the next few days or weeks.

Many artists, although very busy (so ask for only fifteen or twenty minutes of their time or keep your questions to a minimum), are more than willing to talk about how they broke into their field, what worked well, what didn't, and how they continue to pursue sharing their art.

Bonus Prompt! Pick one of the following topics and write for fifteen minutes in your journal:

- Although art is subjective and individual, it is in many ways collective and communal. How do you feel about sharing your art? Does it make a difference if the audience is large or small? What excites you about sharing your work? What is a little overwhelming or confusing?

- Do you think an artist should create what the market seems to want or, instead, create only what the artist feels called or inspired to make? Might the two (market/audience and inspiration) ever overlap in the photos we make?

- Napoleon's toothbrush and other products or belongings of famous people frequently fetch astronomical prices, merely because of the person/group who owned them. What kind of audience would be interested in your photography and/or writing merely because you've created it? Make a list of encouragers—don't forget anyone you know, from your alma mater, your babysitter, community or religious organizations, your mail carrier, to you name it.

Art, Publication, and the M-Word Self-Assessment

There are no right-or-wrong answers to this inventory. The primary purpose of answering these questions is to excavate your own motivations and views on the purpose of your photography as well as how you feel about the possibilities of publishing and/or making money from your photography.

Note that not all photographers believe their artwork should become their employment, and that's perfectly fine. The questions were tailored to help you decide if publishing and monetizing your art are your goals or if you have other, equally meaningful reasons for taking photos.

This inventory may also help you to decide where you want to put more attention as you continue to take photos, whether that means starting to submit work to literary magazines, kick-starting a small photography business, never sending work to magazines that don't pay, participating in or organizing an art show, taking a photography class, or deciding that money shouldn't enter into it and you want to continue to take photos for the pure joy of it. At the least, these questions will create an important dialogue about our expectations and hopes for our work.

My views on making money from my photos most closely resemble (choose one):

- Artists should always be paid, even if it's a token payment like a complimentary issue.

- It's okay if my photos don't receive payment. I just want more people to see them.

- I'm happy to share some photos for free for a while, but eventually I plan to make some money from my photography skills.

- It's okay if my personal-project photos never make money, but I plan to launch a concurrent side business in portrait or wedding photography to bring in the bucks.

- Making photos and making money should never be used in the same sentence. Art is its own reward. I have a day-job or familial resources, such as investments, to make money. My photography is for me.

- Money? What's that, dahling? I'm an artiste! I can't be bothered to think of such matters.

The amount of money I think is fair to be paid for use of one of my photos online/digital rights is _____. (If uncertain, make a guesstimate and research going rates later.)

The amount of money I think is fair to be paid for a photo print is _____. (If uncertain, make a guesstimate and research going rates later.)

The person or group I take photos for most often is:

- **Me, myself, and I:** There's nothing like grabbing my camera and heading off for a new adventure. Many times, I keep my shots to myself, and that's how I like it.

- **Family and friends:** I enjoy their comments on my work, and it's fun to document events and gatherings.

- **Everybody and anybody:** New subjects are everywhere, and I enjoy posting and sharing on social media so that more people have access to my inspiration.

- **My class or workshop:** I find that other artists are the only ones who really get what I'm trying to accomplish with imagery, so I tend to share only with other creative people.

- **Literary magazines**

- **My online following:** such as on Instagram

- **Clients**

- **None of the above**

- **All, or most, of the above**

The category publishers would most likely rank my photos as would be:

- **Amateur:** I'm starting out or have never taken a class, and I'm cool with that. There's plenty to learn, and I can't wait! This book is a great start. (By the way, many publishers of small literary magazines love to give new and skilled amateur photographers a shot—everyone starts somewhere.)

- **Skilled amateur:** I've been shooting for months or years and picking up tips as I go that really enhance my photos compared to where I started. I've started networking with other photographers to increase my knowledge base or I've begun to read books, articles, and magazines with photography tips. I'm thinking about submitting some work soon.

- **Intermediate:** I've participated in an art show or had my work published, either online or in print. Or, I've had my work critiqued or workshopped. Or, I've taken some photography courses in a classroom online or at a school or participated in a photo group for a while.

- **Professional:** While this ranking is highly subjective, it might include working for or owning a photo studio, shooting weddings or engagements or senior portraits, being the featured artist, winning art awards at shows, earning an advanced degree in photography, shooting newborn or children's portraits, and more.

I've received comments and/or compliments on my photos:

- Yes, from people I know

- Yes, from a variety of people, including those online I've never met

- Yes, but I didn't see what the fuss was about

- Nope. Still waiting

- No, but who cares about others' opinions, anyway? If you want to make art, make it!

The thought of publication makes me:

- **Feel excited:** Publishing my work is another great way to share my artistic vision.

- **Feel anxious or queasy:** You never know what they'll do to your photos once they're online or in a print magazine.

- **Pause to ponder if I really want to bother.**

- **Pause to plan how I can accomplish it.**

- **Feel a mixture of various emotions:** such as __
_____.

My dream publication to submit work to is: ____
_____. (Feel free to browse for some fun ones after taking this survey. Type it up and keep it near your computer. That might well become your submission list!)

My artistic themes include (choose all that apply):

- Unique or gritty views of life that may surprise or shock some audiences.

- Cute or cozy domestic images that will soothe many audiences.

- Old-school imagery inspired by some of the world's earliest photographers.

- Flowers, and trees, and sunsets, oh yes!

- Action shots!

- The human body.

- Places and architecture, whether scenic vistas or sophisticated, urban landscapes.

- A hybrid that I'm making my own. For instance, using text atop a photograph or writing haiku poems overtop an image, called *haiga*.

- I don't really have a theme. I just click away at whatever calls to me on a particular day.

If I were going to share my photos, the best fit feels like (pick 1-3 options):

- **Social media:** such as Facebook or Twitter

- **Instagram**

- **Local art shows:** such as at high schools, colleges, and hospitals

- **On my own webpage or blog:** where I could share a larger variety of my photos over time

- **In a guest blog or at a free-stock site:** like Unsplash.com, where my work is part of a wider, more diverse collection by many artists

- **In a self-published, print-art book**

- **In a small, online literary magazine**

- **In a print literary magazine or anthology**

- **On cute products:** like coffee mugs and t-shirts, where the photos can be blended with other design elements

- **Share?** What is this share you speak of? I make art entirely for my own relaxation and enjoyment

My photos are primarily (rank each statement as: 1- *I 100% agree*, 2- *I somewhat agree*, 3- *Who, me? Nope.*):

- **For the joy of making something:** If it's an art form, I'm all over it. Creativity's alive and thriving!

- **To inspire my writing:** Photo imagery and writing imagery share a lot of qualities and skills. My photography sharpens my writing, and I love that.

- **A way to get out of the house, socialize, and expand my friend network:** Photography is a common ground to share with others.

- **A private hobby:** If others enjoy them from time to time, great! But mostly I take them to relax and de-stress.

- **My way to document my life, my children/ grandchildren/nieces/nephews/friends.**

- **Write your own below** _____
_____

Agree or disagree? I would be likely to share more of my art if I knew it wouldn't be criticized by internet trolls.

Agree or disagree? I would be likely to share more of my art if I knew it wouldn't be criticized or misunderstood by people I know, such as friends and family or coworkers.

Agree or disagree? My primary motivation for making photos is internal, such as the good feeling from having taken a shot that I think is more skilled than any I've taken before or taking shots at a new location. Photography brings me closer to myself.

Agree or disagree? My primary motivation for making photos is external, such as sharing with others one-on-one or en-masse online. Photography brings me closer to others.

Agree or disagree? I would be more likely to submit my photos to a literary magazine that offers payment or contributor's copies?

Agree or disagree? I would rather share my art in literary magazines than public venues where artist participation is often encouraged or expected, such as art shows or classroom/guest-speaker talks.

Agree or disagree? If my photography is rejected, I will likely not send art to any publication again. Why keep knocking on a closed door?

Agree or disagree? If my photography is rejected, it will be disappointing, but I understand that art criticism is highly subjective. After I've licked my wounds, I'm likely to give it a go again, perhaps with a different art show, magazine, or contest.

Agree or disagree? I would rather have a smaller audience of people I know personally who support my photography than a large audience of followers, many of whom I might not know?

Agree or disagree? When it comes to my audience, the more the merrier! I'm aiming for thousands of followers and likes for my photos.

Agree or disagree? I feel comfortable taking time away from my photography and writing to do more social networking, launch a website, blog to promote my work, launch a business, and other crucial marketing legwork?

Agree or disagree? If you agree with the last question, about how much time per week (in hours) can you invest in marketing?

Ask yourself:

How much time per week (in hours) can you invest in your photography?

What time or day each week will you assign to marketing?

What time or day each week will you assign to creating new photo content?

If you want to submit your work to literary magazines, art shows, or contests, what day and time of the week or month will you assign to researching markets, preparing your submissions and sending them, and communicating with editors or publishers?

Tips for Writing Fabulous Writer/ Artist Bios

Never published? No problem! Many editors are looking for fresh artistic outlooks. Published in one genre but not any/many others? Again, don't let that stop you from submitting fresh work in any genre.

In the writer/artist bio (sometimes called the artist's statement), you should include details about what makes you a unique person and what inspires your art.

What should you include in your bio if you've never published?

- **Where you're from or where you live.**

- **Your job(s):** readers like to know your vocation, even if it's not related to art of writing, perhaps especially if it's unrelated! Many of us have held five or more jobs that few people know about, some of them quite quirky occupations, too. Not a lot of people know that I worked as a sheet-music librarian for a choir directress for four semesters, that I tutored both Yugoslavian and Japanese business executives in conversational English, or that I was a house-sitter/dog walker and, yes, even a goat caretaker. Such genuine details make you authentically who *you* are. Editors and readers/viewers dig that.

- **Where you went to school or learned about this type of art:** Don't have an arts school diploma? No problem; there are self-taught artists as well as there are university-trained ones, both are valid.

- **A statement about artists or writers whose work has informed or inspired yours:** (This is especially handy if you've never published before or are new to publishing a certain genre of work and need another detail or two to flesh out your bio.)

- **A detail or two about your other hobbies:** Avid gardener? Have the best *coq au vin* this side of Paris? Enjoy antiquing and have a vintage marble collection? These kinds of details make you appear well-rounded to readers/viewers.

- **Are you a dog mom or a cat dad?** How about human children/grandchildren, a spouse, darling nieces and nephews, or a love of your life? Yeah, you can mention those people who support your art and make your world.

- **Had a special event or a milestone (artistically-related or not) recently?** List it.

- **Were there any specific circumstances or unique experiences as you created your imagery?** Feel free to include that. Or perhaps something sparked your photograph or poem, story, or article, such as an event you attended or a movie or a song—note that inspiration. One art form often sparks another.

A few general guidelines to keep in mind when writing your artist statement:

- **Keep your details specific but not longwinded:** If you have been published, list other work within the genre you're submitting and any honors within the past two or three years.

- **Always check the guidelines** for literary magazines and art shows, to see if they ask for specific types of information. Some will want just fifty words or under, while others want bios as long as you care to write. Never write more than what editors and curators request.

- **Match your tone to the tone of the editor and/or published work:** Some editors like third-person, professional bios only (in which case, you'd list your education, your jobs, your website and/or blog, and any publications or other artists who inspire you) while others don't want any professional details but instead appreciate humor and down-to-earth details (in which case, mentioning your family, pets, and milestones would be perfect). If a publication doesn't include many guidelines about the tone of the bio, then you are usually free to mix-and-match professional details with more personal ones.

- It can be fun and insightful to **peruse an issue starting with reading most of the contributors' bios** to see what style other artists/writers have chosen.

Here are two samples of bios that I've used for cover letters, to give you a template and some ideas for how you might craft your own.
The first publication (where I submitted photography) wanted bios that were under one hundred and fifty words. Mine is one hundred and four words and combines my professional, recent book and photo publications, and forthcoming work:

Melanie Faith is an English professor, a tutor at a college-preparatory school, and a freelance writing consultant. In the past two years, her photography has been featured in Minute Magazine, Chantwood Magazine, OVS Magazine, Peacock Journal, Birmingham Arts Journal, Cargo Literary Journal, Door is a Jar, *and* Sandy River Review. *Her photography is forthcoming from Fourth & Sycamore. Her historical poetry collection will be published by FutureCycle Press (fall 2017) and a craft book about writing flash fiction and nonfiction will be published by Vine Leaves Press in spring 2018. She is a winner of the Brain Mill Press Driftless Unsolicited Cover Art Contest.*

This bio is under seventy-five words and was sent with a short story I wrote to a literary magazine. It includes both a detail about my education and a fun last sentence about my other, non-literary interests. Notice the change in tone between the previous bio and this one:

> ***Melanie Faith's*** *writing has been nominated for three Pushcart Prizes. She finds joy writing and teaching in several genres, including poetry, creative nonfiction, flash fiction, flash nonfiction, and instructional/craft articles about the writing process. She holds an MFA in creative writing from Queens University of Charlotte, N.C. In her free time, she collects quotes, books, and shoes; learns about still-life photography and the Tiny-House movement; and travels to spend time with her darling nieces.*

I tend to update my bio every two or three months, taking out older details or details that don't match the kind of writing or photographs I'm submitting. My photo-submission bios tend to focus more on my visual images, although I slide in details about my written books, too, and vice versa.

Here's the bio I submitted with my cover letter last week to *Gulf Stream Literary Magazine*. If you have a website, online portfolio, and/or social media, make sure to list it/them, as I do:

> *Melanie Faith is an English professor, tutor, auntie, and photographer. She sometimes teaches online with a mug of tea and chocolate at the ready. She loves visiting the Butterfly Palace with her darling nieces.*

This spring, she's teaching a dream class she created: Photography for Writers. Recent publications include a poetry collection, This Passing Fever *(FutureCycle Press, September 2017), and two forthcoming craft books for writers, called* In a Flash *and* Poetry Power *(both from Vine Leaves Press, 2018). Read more about her writing, photography, and publications at:* melaniedfaith.com/blog

Submitting Your Work to Literary Magazines & Other Venues Looking for Photos:

Cover Letter Tips:

A cover letter is the first glimpse an editor gets into your artistic presentation. Make sure to proofread your prose for the first impression before submitting, but don't bite your knuckles over what to include.

Think of the cover letter as a chance to introduce yourself to editors and staff, to get them excited about the writing and/or photography you've submitted, and then let your artwork itself shine.

What elements go into a good cover letter?

- **List the titles of the work you're submitting and the word-length** (if poetry or prose). **List titles of photographs** and/or note how many photos you are sending in the submission.

- **If you've read their publication** (online, in print, or both) **or are a subscriber**, mention so!

- **Include a brief author/artist's bio.**

- **Note if you are sending your photos or writing to another publication at the same time** (called a "simultaneous submission" or "simult. sub."). Before submitting, make sure you read their guidelines first to make sure they accept simultaneous submissions; **the majority of publications do, but don't assume so.**

- **Include your contact information** (email, website, and/or phone number).

- **Always end by thanking them.** Most literary magazines and galleries get thousands of submissions for a dozen or fewer spots, so it's a big deal that they spent time to consider your work, even if they can't use it in this issue.

One of the best ways to learn how to write a cover letter is to have an example. Here's a recent cover letter I sent for my nonfiction craft-article submission (which was published in May 2018).

Dear Fiction Southeast Editors and Staff,

I read your call for submissions for articles about the writing life, and I wish to submit my own original and unpublished article that has ~1740 words. The title of my craft article is: 'Writer in Progress: The Writer's Idea Book, Submission Notebook, and You.'

I have attached my article as a PDF file.

As per your posted guidelines, here is a short biographical statement about me and my artistic background/writing: Melanie Faith is an English professor, a tutor at a college-preparatory school, and a freelance writing consultant. Her photography is forthcoming from Fourth & Sycamore. Her historical poetry collection was published by FutureCycle Press (fall 2017) amazon.com/dp/B075CP1CNP and a craft book about writing flash fiction and nonfiction will be published by Vine Leaves Press in spring 2018. She is a 2017 winner of the Brain Mill Press Driftless Unsolicited Cover Art Contest. For more about her writing and photography, check out: melaniedfaith.com.

Thank you for your time and kind consideration of my work. Please note that I have other articles pertaining to the writing life, should that be of interest to you. Should you have any questions about my submission at any time, please feel free to contact me. Best,

Melanie Faith

Please note that the examples I provide in this chapter are cover letters I emailed. The vast majority of query and cover letters are now emailed, but now and again publications prefer formal, printed and mailed letter format. A printed query would follow a slightly stricter format, opening instead with my name and contact information, and then the date, and finally, my publication's name and contact information before the body of the cover letter.

Here's another cover letter that I sent when I submitted photography from a series in August 2017, which were published subsequently. (Check out the PDF photo file at melaniedfaith.com/photography-for-writers for photos #17, #18, #19, and #20.)

The market's guidelines asked to know about the origin of our photos and the series concept in general, so you'll find details about that in this letter as well; sometimes magazines don't ask for these details, especially for fiction and poetry submissions or for photographs that are not part of an ongoing series.

Always read contest, literary magazine, and galleries' guidelines and follow them to a "T." Sometimes, great work is rejected due to not following instructions, which is a shame.

Dear Editors and Staff,

I wish to submit five of my own, original and unpublished photos from my 'Iseult' series for your kind consideration. The names of my attached photos are: 'Iseult: Curls,' 'Iseult, Homecoming,' 'Iseult—Layers,' 'Iseult—Like a Hundred Years ago was Yesterday,' and 'Iseult—Ruffles and Repose.'

The name of this series is based on the medieval Irish princess from the tale of Tristan and Iseult (also often spelled Isolde), a tale of serendipity and romance on one hand and great vulnerability and tragedy on the other.

While the clothing used for this photo shoot comes

from a much more modern time period (including the white dress from the 1930s and a grey evening gown), my fascination with historical elements as well as what parts of the human spirit remain timeless—melancholy, reflection, silent hopes, reunion—are a backdrop for the creation process as are the literary degrees I've earned and my interest in compressed imagery as a poet and writer.

Most of my photography publications have been still-life, nature, or architectural tableau, so this series was a wonderful way to exert different muscles while working with my camera and a model—from conception of ideas to the possibilities and limits of the human form to the happy surprises that occur when creative minds work in unison with each other. Another meaningful aspect of this series was working with my sister, who was visiting from far away. It was an exciting challenge to bring to my compositions my sister's qualities that I know well and appreciate as well as newer elements of her personality that underscore meaning as a series.

Here is a biographical statement as well as a statement about my art: Melanie Faith is an English professor, a tutor at a college-preparatory school, and a freelance writing consultant. In the past two years, her photography has been featured in Minute Magazine, Chantwood Magazine, OVS Magazine, Peacock Journal, Birmingham Arts Journal, Cargo Literary Journal, Door is a Jar, and Sandy River Review. *Her historical poetry collection will be published by FutureCycle Press (fall 2017) and a craft book about writing flash fiction and nonfiction will be published by Vine Leaves Press in spring 2018. She is a 2017 winner of the Brain Mill Press Driftless Unsolicited Cover Art Contest. brainmillpress.com/books/a-wife-is-a-hope-chest*

Please note that I plan for these photos to be simultaneous submissions. Should my work be accepted elsewhere, I will contact you immediately; I also have other photos in the series, should those be of interest.

I have paid my $25 entrance fee via PayPal. Should you have any questions or concerns about my submission, please feel free to contact me at any time. Thank you for your time and kind consideration of my work.

Best,

Melanie Faith

Image-Making Resources to Check Out!

Websites:

- Art Deadline.com: artdeadline.com

- A wonderful, free listing of galleries looking for themed photography for shows, print or online journals seeking work, contests, and more. Bookmark this one for return visits of updated artist calls and opportunities.

- ***Black & White* (B&W) *Magazine*:** bandwmag. com

- **CreateWriteNow:** Wonderful articles on the power of journaling from a variety of evocative literary voices as well as motivating courses, books, videos, and mentoring with bestselling author of *Journaling Power: How to Create the Happy, Healthy Live You Want to Live,* Mari L. McCarthy. createwritenow.com

- **Instagram:** instagram.com

- Endless, evolving inspiration at your fingertips. Here are a few of my favorite feeds; feel free to use these hashtags as a jumping-off point for finding your own go-to curated pages. #gloomandglow #fridayfacelessportrait #createeveryday #artistsoninstagram #creativelifehappylife #createinspirepositivity #dontquityourdaydream #bookgeek #noiretblanc #blackandwhitephotography #seekthesimplicity #simplethingsmadebeautiful #stilllife_perfection #slowliving #aquietstyle #moodygrams #mystillsundaycompetition #noiretblancphotographie #everysquareastory #wetplatecollodion #momentsofmine #lightandshadow

- **Kim Klassen.com:** kimklassen.com

- A few years ago, I took an online photography seminar with Canadian still-life artist Kim Klassen (see a link to her Instagram, inspired podcast, pre-sets for photographers, and classes below). Last fall, I took a journaling class with her that was creativity boosting.

- The Lomographic Society International: lomography.com

- Pinterest: pinterest.com/despotronminet/ombre-et-lumi%C3%A8re

- While there are thousands of possibilities for inspirational feeds, one of my favorites for literary and photographic spurring is a page of thematic photographs of light and shadow, called **"ombre et lumière."** Within a short while of perusing, it's likely you'll find many of your own favorite themes and subjects represented on pages you'll follow to or bookmark for future inspiration.

- **SHOTS Magazine:** shotsmag.com

- I've subscribed to this black-and-white photo magazine for about ten years now, but it's been published for over thirty-two years. Wonderful variety of innovative fine-arts imagery, between figure studies, landscape work, still-life, and more. Just came under new ownership last year with Douglas Beasley.

Creativity/Craft Books:

- *Zen and the Art of Photography: A Guide to Mindfulness in Creativity* by Douglas Beasley: douglasbeasley.com/zen-the-art-of-photography-book

- *Writing from the Senses: 59 Exercises to Ignite Creativity and Revitalize Your Writing* by Laura Deutsch

- *The Photographer's Playbook* by Jason Fulford and Gregory Halpern, Editors

- *Will Write for Food: The Complete Guide to Writing Cookbooks, Blogs, Memoir, Recipes, and More* by Dianne Jacob

- *The Flower Can Always Be Changing* by Shawna

Lemay: Evocative and engaging essays on artmaking, life-living and the intersection of inspiration and wonder. Shawna also writes the popular and always-inspiring writing, photography, and creativity blog, Transactions with Beauty at transactionswithbeauty.com as well as an excellent novel, Rumi and the Red Handbag.

- *Word Painting: The Fine Art of Writing Descriptively* by Rebecca McClanahan

- *On Photography* by Susan Sontag

- *Zen Camera: Creative Awakening with a Daily Practice in Photography* by David Ulrich

Artistic Community-Building, Classes, and Miscellaneous Opportunities:

- CreateLive: creativelive.com

- From wedding photography to boudoir, senior portraits and photojournalism to fine-arts, or conceptual portraits and product photography to landscape, nature, and launching a photo-based career, this photo-class company has it all! My parents purchased two of their courses for me for Christmas a few years ago, and I've since bought seven or eight more. Many of the instructors have owned businesses for years and/or worked for leading photographic markets/magazines. While they do offer some free content on air each week as they stream live, the courses are all later available 24/7 for purchase and play-back at your own pace (which is how I've taken the courses). Many classes include invaluable tips for growth as a photographer and image-maker as well as bonus, downloadable content for purchased classes. For free content aired each week, go to: creativelive. com

- **Flickr:** flickr.com

- A free site where you can share your photos, search for photography groups to join, peruse topics, and/or "like" others' photos. If you seek to continue photographing each week or each day, then joining an online group and committing to posting periodically will help you to form community and to grow as a visual artist. While I haven't posted my own work on Flickr in years, I sometimes go to my account to search for images to inspire my writing and/or photoshoots and to see what my favorite image-makers are creating.

- **All Sorts of Lovely:** allsortsoflovely.com

- I took a two-week online class from British life-style photographer and flat-lay expert Emily Quinton five years ago, and it encouraged me to take my image-making to another level by practicing daily and completing challenges, just as I do periodically for my writing practice. This is Emily's 2019-launched website and newsletter.

- Squam: squamartworkshops.com/podcast

- I might have listed this last but it's far from least.

In fact, my sister (knitter and crafter extraordinaire) turned me onto this free podcast from the Squam arts community in Provincetown, Rhode Island. Each episode interviews and follows women making various types of media, their creative passage, rerouting and life circumstances that led to where they are today, and the steps it takes to follow one's bliss and to continue learning one's craft over a lifetime. I'm nerding out over every conversation! They also host workshops and seminars at their arts colony, which I've added to my dream list.

Acknowledgements

The chapter, "Tropey-Dokey: Enhancing Imagery with Tropes," first appeared as a *Women on Writing* Spotlight article.

Books aren't written in a vacuum. I am grateful to the following supporters of my writing whose tireless belief and assistance crafted this project into the volume you hold today:

- Many thanks to my Dream Team at Vine Leaves Press, Jessica Bell and Alexis Paige, for the consistent encouragement, literary advice and edits, amazing cover design, and belief in the value of my craft books. Also, for genuine vision and literary awesomeness. It was an honor to get to work with you both again.

- Kudos and appreciation to Amie McCracken, Vine Leaves Publishing Director, for passionate belief in the quality of all of the Vine Leaves' excellent books and for employing book-marketing talents with Jessica Bell on behalf of gleaning a wider audience for my literary brainchildren.

- Much appreciation to my talented writing friends and beta-readers—Antonia Albany, Kate Bradley-Ferrall, and Kandace "Kandy" Chapple— who read various chapters-in-progress and offered both enthusiasm and stellar suggestions along this writing path. Your support of me as a writer and your belief in this book were unflagging and so motivating. Merci beaucoup! this book's message: Kandy Chapple, Shawna Lemay, and Mari L. McCarthy. I know that it's no easy feat to encapsulate an entire book in a statement, and I am grateful for your thoughtful, focused statements on behalf of this book's content.

- For my parents, Thom and Linda Faith, my stellar sister and brother-in-law, Amanda and Adam McGrath, and my darling nieces, Cora Vi and Sylvie Ro. Your consistent care, love, and support of my writing and photographic paths mean the world to me.

- For my students. You are the real deal, dear fellow scribes and photographers. Sharing time, our work, and this writing and photographing process with you has been one of the ongoing privileges of my professional life. You keep me inspired.

- Last but not least: for you, dear reader. My intention is that this book will be an inspiring companion you'll find good company on your own creative journey.

- Thanks so much to my blurb writers and fellow creative, innovative writers for their endorsement of: Kandy Chapple, Shawna Lemay, and Mari L. McCarthy. I know that it's no easy feat to encapsulate an entire book in a statement, and I am grateful for your thoughtful, focused statements on behalf of this book's content.

- For my parents, Thom and Linda Faith, my stellar sister and brother-in-law, Amanda and Adam McGrath, and my darling nieces, Cora Vi and Sylvie Ro. Your consistent care, love, and support of my writing and photographic paths mean the world to me.

- For my students. You are the real deal, dear fellow scribes and photographers. Sharing time, our work, and this writing and photographing process with you has been one of the ongoing privileges of my professional life. You keep me inspired.

- Last but not least: for you, dear reader. My intention is that this book will be an inspiring companion you'll find good company on your own creative journey.

Vine Leaves Press

Enjoyed this book?
Go to *vineleavespress.com* to find more.

www.ingramcontent.com/pod-product-compliance
Lightning Source LLC
Chambersburg PA
CBHW021617270326
41931CB00008B/735